The Auxiliary Teacher Program:

A Complete Manual and Guide

JERRY L. ABBOTT

Foreword by Dr. Walter B. Barbe

PARKER PUBLISHING COMPANY, INC.
WEST NYACK, NEW YORK

© 1973 *by*

PARKER PUBLISHING COMPANY, INC.

West Nyack, N.Y.

Library of Congress Cataloging in Publication Data

Abbott, Jerry L
   The auxiliary teacher program.

   Bibliography: p.
   1. Teachers' assistants--Handbooks, manuals, etc.
I. Title.
LB2844.1.A8A2   371.1'412   73-4776
ISBN 0-13-054569-4

Printed in the United States of America

To my wife Sandra and my daughter Andrea,
who are the <u>light</u> of my life.

Foreword

The goal of today's school must be to provide for each child the type of education best suited to his particular needs. But if the diverse needs of children are to be met, there is a growing awareness that traditional methods and approaches are not sufficient. The answer is not the addition of more courses of study, or adherence to one prescribed method of instruction. Instead, the answer lies in acceptance of a philosophy of individualized or personalized instruction. The critical problem then becomes the implementation of such a program. In *The Auxiliary Teacher Program*, Jerry Abbott recognizes the problem and explores practical solutions.

This is a book filled with ideas for improving the teacher-learning situation through the use of auxiliary personnel. Previously, aside from urgent cries for additional staffing, little attention has been given to the problem. Here the basis for the effective use of auxiliary personnel is established, with directions for their training and a variety of suitable activities for them to follow. Nowhere else is there as comprehensive a source of such information.

It will become evident that the author knows schools, knows teachers, and knows children. The detailed directions and examples include the kind of reminders and cautions that come only from practical experience, from use in a school situation. The ideas listed at the end of each chapter are simply stated, direct, and practical.

The author's message in this book is a personal one to the reader. Some of the suggestions express ideas the reader shares, but may have never articulated. Some suggestions will leave the reader wondering why he never thought of them before.

The author's premise is that the school has not adequately done the job which it must do. He reinforces it by demonstrating how the teacher-learning situation can be improved through the use of auxiliary personnel.

How can the schools hope to accomplish all the tasks which society places upon them—and meet approval by those to whom the schools must ultimately be accountable, the general public? Many books have been written deploring the job the schools are doing, as have an equal number deploring the impossibility of the task itself. But in this book, *The Auxiliary Teacher Program: A Complete Manual and Guide,* Jerry Abbott offers a solution which works.

Walter B. Barbe
Editor
Highlights for Children

A Word from the Author on the Scope and Purpose of this Book . . . .

For too long we have considered someone to be professional on the basis of training, experience, the status of the university attended, and perhaps the hierarchical arrangement that someone has given the various fields of study.

I am suggesting that educators are truly professional when they are perceptive enough to realize limitations and deal with them in effective ways. This kind of professional comes to the classroom with antennae out, seeking every opportunity to enrich the lives of children. He looks at the task to be accomplished, and decides upon his competency to teach it. If it is within the limits of his training and experience, he will proceed. If not, he will seek help by employing the talents of students, parents, teacher aides, or other resource people of the community.

Team teaching, the innovative staffing plan dedicated to the improvement of instruction in the '60s, was predicated on the assumption that no one person could meet the individual needs of students and the notion that division of labor among professionals (and later aides or para-professionals) made good sense.

Of late, the recognition that communities need and want to be more actively involved in the educational process and decision making related to that process, has created near pandemonium in public schools throughout the country. The recent development of free schools, store-front schools, alternative schools and community schools has reinforced the position that schools simply will not continue to exist as isolated, professionally planned and operated institutions in a rapidly changing society.

The question of teacher teaming is no longer relevant. Teachers cannot by choice operate any longer in isolation as the single expert charged with the responsibility for educating a group of young people.

Educators may choose to ignore the concerns of the clientele taxpayer and preside over the dismemberment and erosion of the once sacred common school system. On the other hand, the opportunity for capitalizing on the growing interest and concern of parents provides a whole new array of human and material resources which could lead the American public school system into a new frontier of productivity and relevance.

Not long ago, I walked into a kindergarten room and observed the following activities:

> As I entered the room, it looked unusually full. There were groups of people spread all over the room and into the halls. One group was working with the classroom teacher on handwriting. Next to her was a student from Intermediate VI helping some children write thank you notes to the Shriners for circus tickets. In another area of the room a student teacher was playing an educational game with a group of children. In the hallway a university aide was working with a group of children on Key Words in reading. Two parents were in the back of the room helping children plant seeds and build birdhouses. Everything was well organized and each group seemed oblivious of what the others were doing (Fig. 1).

As you witness something like this over and over, you cannot help but be impressed by the fact that even though one teacher has been assigned one group, she has managed to implement a team teaching situation.

How do we demonstrate to children our belief that people who live together must also be able to work together? How do we stop so many fine teachers from walking into their classrooms and closing the door behind them?

First, I think we stop the power struggle and allow formal team teaching to proceed at its own rate. Walls can come down only so fast, and teacher readiness to accept hierarchical arrangements will not come about until they feel more secure about their role.

Second, I think it is now time for every front-line educator in America, notwithstanding their school's organization, to organize the teacher's team. And all this means is that they search far and

Two Parents

Student Teacher and Teacher

Kindergarten and the Teacher's Team

University Sophomore Aide

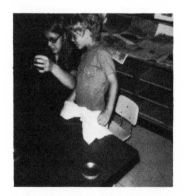

Intermediate VI Tutor

Figure 1

wide for human resources that can help them carry out the tremendously complex set of tasks now required.

How to tap this new resource pool and utilize the many talents and interests available is the focus of this book. This book is written as a guide to help both teachers and administrators to organize and install such a program.

Chapter 1 establishes the need for an auxiliary program and gives guidelines for organizing and evaluating the program. It also discusses the advantages and disadvantages of auxiliaries working in the school.

Chapters 2 and 3 are in-depth discussions of tutor programs. Chapter 2 emphasizes models for tutor programs and an operational plan for a tutor program. Chapter 3 deals almost entirely with tutor training and has application for all auxiliaries.

Chapters 4 and 5 deal with programs of community involvement. Chapter 4 describes a process for launching a successful program. Chapter 5 is a storehouse of ideas on how to take advantage of the many opportunities we have to involve parents.

Chapter 6 is a plan for more relevant ways to report to parents. This chapter is included because our program of community involvement is directly related to our ability to find the entwining relationship with parents. If this cannot be found, all else will fail. It includes a plan for more relevant ways of reporting based upon a four step approach.

Chapter 7 recognizes that auxiliaries, excited as they are about helping in the schools, need effective ideas to help them motivate children. Ideas in the areas of reading, spelling, creative writing, and mathematics are included in abundance.

Since good schools have good leaders, Chapter 8 places the building principal squarely in the middle of all facets of the teacher's team and attempts to gaze into the crystal ball and make some predictions about the future of the principalship.

How will your school be different as a result of using the more than 700 ideas found in this book? Of course, decreasing the pupil-teacher ratio will make it significantly easier to implement new programs, and children will be given a far richer experience through a relationship to people who are teaching to their strengths.

There will be a broader base for decision making as a result of inviting parents to become actively involved in the school. The current debate about the mission of the schools makes it imperative that parents contribute to the decisions that affect their children.

Probably as significant is the fact that public understanding will begin to improve. Through involvement and participation, operation of the schools and the problems faced by schools can be communicated in such a way as to increase public support and stem the tide of rapidly growing apathy and disillusion in the American school system.

If you use the ideas in this book, I guarantee that your school will be different. I wish you well in your efforts to plan, organize, and implement the auxiliary teacher program.

JLA

Acknowledgments

Difficult as it is to credit all of the people who have contributed to this effort, I gratefully acknowledge:

All of the staff members of J. Nelson Kelly Elementary School, whose creative flow didn't stop for the entire six years I worked with them.

Ronald Bommersbach, Jean Brownson, Gerald Cook, Jeanette Ferrie, Clarine Lian, Joyce McCabe, Mary Nudell, Dorothy Sparks and Elizabeth Weeks, for their never-ending implementation of innovative ideas, and for their willingness to share them both with me and the thousands of visitors who viewed our program.

The three superintendents with whom I worked during these six years: Dr. Edwin Cramer, who first tapped any creative potential I might have had; Dr. Wayne Worner, whose genius for innovation gave me a never ending supply of ideas; and Dr. Richard Hill, who encouraged and sustained my work.

Former Assistant Superintendent of Schools, Dr. Donald Mrdjenovich, for the support he gave our program and for having so much faith in my ideas that he let me try them on his new staff at Watertown, Wisconsin.

Assistant Superintendent of Schools, Dr. Harold Bergquist, whose ideas frequent this book, and for his readiness to help and support the J. Nelson Kelly school program whenever it needed it.

Margaret Abbott, who for six years was the director of the Grand Forks Teacher Aide Project. Her ideas permeate this book.

The Grand Forks Principals Council, for the many debates we have had, and the way those debates helped shape my thinking.

To my former interns, Larry Hoiberg and Andrew Swanson, for our many discussions about education, and their never-ending sharing of ideas, many of which are found in this book.

The hundreds of parents at J. Nelson Kelly Elementary School who allowed themselves to become deeply involved in the school program.

The two educators who have most influenced my educational philosophy, Dr. Walter B. Barbe, Editor of *Highlights for Children,* and Mrs. Norma Randolph, Executive Vice President in Charge of Program Development, Self-Enhancing Education, Inc.

My secretary, Mrs. Elaine Laursen, for her help with the manuscript, and her very able leadership in administering our auxiliary program for all of the six years.

Finally, to my wife Sandra, for her constant help and encouragement, and her understanding as I retreated to my den each night.

Table of Contents

Chapter 7—Effective Activities for Auxiliaries to Use with Children *(Continued)*

> *. Effective writing ideas . Effective ideas in mathematics . Effective use of the tape recorder*

> *How the principal relates to the teacher's team . The principal's team*

Chapter 1

The Auxiliary Program
as a First Step to Action

It is no secret that many of the nation's teachers spend valuable time performing tasks that require little professional competence and responsibility. Neither is it a secret that this is negatively affecting educational programs everywhere.

Why is that? Why should highly trained teachers want to continue counting money, supervising playgrounds, and running the duplicating machine? Because change is frightening and upsetting to many people. Continued involvement in all sorts of peripheral activities provides a convenient barrier against change.

At the present time, thousands of the nation's teachers are trapped in this web of hopelessness. Elementary teachers are busy supervising children from the time they come to school in the morning until they go home at night. Secondary teachers oftentimes go beyond that. It is not uncommon for secondary teachers and administrators to spend countless hours supervising athletic events, riding buses to and from contests, and organizing and administering a myriad of clubs and organizations. To allow this to continue is to perpetrate a crime against the children of America. The supervisor that lets this happen at the expense of the instructional program should be severely reprimanded at best, and maybe relieved of his leadership responsibilities.

So there are two groups of teachers and administrators—those spending a good deal of their time bogged down in clerical duties and liking it, and those spending a good deal of their time bogged down in clerical duties and not liking it.

What can be done about it? First, schools must begin organizing auxiliary programs at once. Second, they must also begin programs of in-service in an effort to help teachers and administrators deal with the problems of change.

The last ten years or so have seen a great movement in the area of auxiliary help for the classroom teacher. In far too many instances this auxiliary help has been limited to teacher aides. Today programs are beginning to recognize that other auxiliaries exist and are slowly enlisting the help of parents, students, and university personnel as well as the paid teacher aide.

A Warning

As early as 1966, and probably before that, concerned educators were warning of the effects of changing school programs without concomitant changes in the role of the teacher. George Denmark, in the March 1968 issue of the *National Education Association Journal,* in an article entitled, "The Teacher and His Staff," writes:

> The job of today's teacher has become virtually unmanageable. Unless something is done to remedy the situation, creative, competent teachers will find themselves hopelessly bogged down in technical and clerical duties which could be performed by others. Or they will be overwhelmed by so many complex and important things to do that few if any of the tasks will be done well enough to leave them with any sense of accomplishment.
> America's children will be cheated out of the quality education they deserve. Curricula will be standardized rather than individualized because schools keep their teachers busy collecting money, recording attendance, and supervising lunchrooms, instead of counseling with students, planning learning experiences with colleagues, and analyzing recent teaching efforts.[1]

[1] "The Teacher and His Staff " (Washington, D.C.: *National Education Journal,* March, 1968), p. 17.

It is pretty difficult to say it much better than that. Meaningful program change is simply not going to take place to any degree unless there is an all-out effort to change the role of the teacher.

Others Are Doing It

The last several years have seen a tremendous growth in auxiliary programs in professions other than education. Doctors, dentists and nurses are examples of professions that have separated non-professional tasks from professional ones. It is a rare doctor that gives shots to patients, or nurses who make beds. Extreme shortages in these professions, together with a thorough understanding of professional role, have no doubt been the reason for this giant step forward.

Not long ago, the New York City mayor discovered, much to his amazement, that eleven hundred policemen, all well-trained, were providing clerical services. These men were immediately transferred to positions which took greater advantage of their training, skills and experience. Non-professional personnel are now performing many of the duties previously performed by these well-trained officers.[2]

Teachers Can Do It, Too

Slowly the teaching profession is beginning to realize the importance of the changed role of the teacher. Creative leadership in the schools, together with the tremendous thrust of the Teacher Educational and Professional Standards, beginning in 1966 with the *Year Of The Non Conference,* has made the changed role of the teacher a reality in many places. It is now estimated that between 200,000 and 300,000 teacher aides are now working in the nation's schools.[3]

The teaching profession probably has more resources available to it than any other profession. No other profession has such a large and varied clientele. The range of resources is legion. Too

---

[2]Milton Wartenberg, *An Understanding of the Role of Auxiliary Personnel in Education Series,* Unit One (Chicago, Ill.: Science Research Associates, Inc., 1967), p. 1.

[3]Beatrice M. Gudridge, *Paraprofessionals in Schools: How the New Careerists Bolster Education* (Washington, D.C.: National School Public Relations Association, 1972), p. 1.

often we think only of the paid teacher aide. Every parent in the nation is a potential resource. So are many people who are not parents. Students teaching students is yet in its infancy. The resources that reside in our nation's colleges and universities are a huge, untapped reservoir.

Educators are on the move. Auxiliary programs are springing up. Increasingly, teachers are beginning to find new resources to enrich their classroom. All that is needed now is an increased pace.

Do Teachers Want to Do It?

Most evidence still seems to indicate that the greatest deterrent to the use of auxiliaries in schools is the teacher. In a recent study by the National School Public Relations Association, called *Paraprofessionals in Schools: How New Careerists Bolster Education,* it was found that:

> The spread of the paraprofessional movement is hindered not only by a shortage of funds, but by lingering fears of teachers who still feel threatened by the new position.[4]

The report further found that teachers, although losing some of their fears about aide programs implemented during the sixties, still have a "residue of doubt."

Margaret Abbott, former director of the Grand Forks, North Dakota Teacher Aide Project, when asked about the problems of implementing auxiliary programs, said about the same thing: Teachers are still hesitant to relinquish many of the duties formerly thought to be theirs. Teacher aides often report they are treated more like maids than aides.

So the teacher, it appears, is underestimating the potential of the auxiliary. What can be done about that? In the above study by the National School Public Relations Association they suggested that training programs need to be developed. Teachers need to know how to use this *new army of helpers.*

Part of this training must center around human relations training. Teachers need to know new communication skills, now that they are leaving the confines of the self-contained classroom and entering into close relationships with others.

---

[4]Gudridge, *Paraprofessionals in Schools,* p. 39.

Educational Changes That Necessitate the Changed Role

Never have so many things been asked of the classroom teacher. And the future doesn't look much brighter in terms of decreasing the scope of the responsibilities of the teacher. Following are some educational and cultural changes that have made the changed role of the teacher an imperative:

A. School Organization

There is a steady movement away from the self-contained classroom. This creates a great increase in activities such as planning for instruction with other adults and the learning of new communication skills.

B. New Curriculum

Hardly a day goes by that some new program is not produced. To become familiar with all of these new materials places a great strain on the classroom teacher.

C. Homemade Curriculum

Increasingly, school systems are developing curriculum locally. The time and energy necessary to undertake such tasks absolutely requires the professionalization of education.

D. Federal Funds

Federal programs have brought more materials into our schools than we ever dreamed possible. This material sits unused in many schools because no one has the time to study it carefully.

E. Technology in Education

Technology has the same potential to relieve teachers of non-professional tasks as does a human auxiliary program. Technology in education will never reach its potential if teachers are not free to examine it.

F. Accountability

Today, as never before, teachers are being held accountable for what they teach. Accountability, with its emphasis upon every child reaching his potential, makes the changed role of the teacher imperative.

G.   Record Keeping

Innovative programs seem to necessitate an increased reliance upon careful records. Time-consuming record keeping, if done by the classroom teacher, will defeat the very thing the program is trying to accomplish.

H.   Transience

The rate at which people, places, and things pass through our lives is increasing.[5] The complexity of life in general makes it imperative that teachers find personnel to help them carry out many of their functions.

What Is an Auxiliary Program?

To many educators, an auxiliary program is simply dividing up. the staff by some reasonable number and assigning them teacher aides. This is not an auxiliary program. In fact, it may result in thwarting any auxiliary program that might be developed later.

An auxiliary program is a concerted effort on the part of a given school or school system to harness all of the available resources within the district, and make them function in a coordinated manner for the benefit of all of the children of that school or district. It further implies that the program will be so organized as to effect the changed role of the teacher to the degree that they can give their total effort to diagnosis, managing learning experiences, and decision making.

Model for an Auxiliary Program

The changed role of the teacher will be accomplished only if there is a concentrated effort to harness all of the resources available to a school.

It is therefore very important that each school try to develop its own model for effecting the very best kind of program. This model

---

[5] Alvin Toffler, *Future Shock* (New York, N.Y.: Random House, Inc., 1971), p. 46.

Model For An Auxiliary Program

Principal

School Secretary	Teachers or Teaching Teams	Principal
Teacher Aides (clerical)	University Aides and Tutors	University Staff
Students	Teacher Aides (instructional)	Classes From the University
Secretary	Parents	Special Parent Groups
Volunteer Parents	Student Teachers	Students of Other Cultures
_____	Future Teachers of America	Visitors
_____	_____	Educators on Sabbatical

CLERICAL STRAND   SPECIAL STRAND
   (A)   INSTRUCTIONAL STRAND (B)   (C)
        THE CHANGED ROLE OF THE TEACHER
          IMPROVEMENT OF INSTRUCTION

Figure 1-1

calls for every member of the faculty to look closely at the tasks he is performing. In the past it had been common to assign teacher aides many of the clerical tasks that were formerly done by teachers, only to find that in some instances the teacher aide could outperform the teacher. So there is a need to look at the total educational experience of a given school. If the teacher aide has a college degree and several years of experience, it would be a mistake to have her spend a lot of time cutting letters for bulletin boards. There are other members of the auxiliary staff that can be assigned to this duty.

What should the model look like? First, it seems appropriate that the building principal be the overall coordinator of the auxiliary program. Directly responsible to him might be the school secretary, who would have total responsibility for the clerical strand of the program. The individual teachers or teams of teachers would, out of necessity, be responsible for the instructional strand of the program, and the principal himself might take total responsibility of the special strand of the program.

The clerical strand is that part of the program that handles all requests for clerical work (A). Every request comes to the school secretary and she decides who is most appropriate for the task. If the request is something of a confidential nature, she might do it herself. If not, she could assign it to a clerical aide, students from within or outside the building, or volunteer parents. The key, of course, is that the classroom teacher never spends any time doing this sort of thing, nor does a highly trained or highly skilled teacher aide or parent volunteer who may want to work directly with children in the classroom.

The instructional strand, to be effective, must be in the hands of the teachers (B). University aides, tutors, and student teachers, for the best results, are directly assigned to classroom teachers. Instructional aides and parents who wish to work in the classroom are also assigned directly.

The special strand of the program is that unknown that must, of necessity, be totally in the hands of the building principal (C). The members of this strand are university or college professors who may wish to work with teachers and pupils on occasion, or college classes, which on demand might want to come into the school and teach lessons in various subjects. It could also mean the scheduling of resource persons from around the community or people from other cultures, such as foreign students at universities. Because this strand is always an unknown, the principal feeds it into the school program whenever there is a demand for a particular kind of service.

If this model is implemented in an organized way, only one thing can result—the changed role of the teacher and the improvement of instruction. Done poorly it can lead to confusion and finally disuse.

The sample model presented here works best in a college or university setting. However, the idea of setting up a model for an auxiliary program will work anywhere, only the components will be different.

The key to a sound auxiliary program is that all components of the program focus on appropriate tasks. Following are some examples of jobs to be done and appropriate personnel for those jobs:

A.	Work in the library	(volunteer parents)
B.	Cutting letters for bulletin boards	(elementary students)
C.	Putting test scores on cardex	(school secretary)
D.	Duplicating worksheets	(clerical aide)
E.	Scheduling a resource person	(principal)
F.	Making instructional games	(parent aides)
G.	Working with a small group	(instructional aide)
H.	Tutoring one child	(student)
I.	Planning for instruction	(teaching teams)
J.	Small group work	(student teacher)

Of course, this list is not meant to imply that only one facet of an auxiliary staff can do a specific job. Rather, it is meant to imply that a constant effort needs to be made to coordinate the task to be done with the staff to do it. If this effort is not made, it is sure to result in a lot of wasted effort by a lot of well-trained, talented personnel.

Entry Skills of Auxiliaries

What kinds of skills should auxiliaries have? Should they have had experience teaching children? Should they have raised children? Should they have had some formal training after high school?

In an auxiliary program as varied as the one described, there is no formal route that is needed to be part of that auxiliary program. Anyone can, in some way, be a contributing member of such a program. However, there are some basic qualities that have been found to be very beneficial in working with children. They are:

Emotional Stability
Fondness for Children
Positive Attitude About Life
Enthusiasm
Ability to Relate to Children and Adults
Good Health
No Ethnic Prejudice [6]

[6] Margaret Abbott, *Teacher Aide Training: Grand Forks, North Dakota* (Grand Forks, North Dakota: 1970), p. 6.

Given these skills, auxiliaries will succeed with other adults and with children. Of course other competencies, such as formal training in teaching, knowledge of office machines, and typing ability, are additional talents that will help them do their job better.

Problems of Having Auxiliaries in Your School

Whenever a teacher leaves her sacred portal and enters into all sorts of team relationships with many other adults, problems are sure to result. Following are some of the problems that have developed in auxiliary programs and perhaps can be avoided if understood and discussed:

A. People who work together must plan together. When they don't, confusion and discontent will result.

B. Some auxiliaries need training before they can meaningfully contribute to a certain aspect of the classroom. The classroom teacher, teaching teams, and the total school staff must have an on-going in-service program if children are to receive the optimum benefits of the program.

C. Teachers oftentimes think too narrowly of what auxiliaries can do. In-service programs with teachers must be on-going to alleviate this condition.

D. Adults who work in close relationship with other adults will place strain on human relationships. Programs need to be implemented that will help adults relate to each other in more entwining ways.

E. Constant efforts must be made to ask auxiliaries for feedback. Failure to do so will lead them to believe that they are the bottom rung of a complex hierarchy.

F. State laws or local policies sometimes restrict the use of auxiliaries.

G. Teacher organizations and unions may feel threatened by the advance of a group whom they feel may take their jobs.

H. There may be a tendency for auxiliaries to be given the toughest assignments. Constant effort and careful assessment are needed to assure that this doesn't happen.

I. At the present time nearly all auxiliaries are women. Efforts are needed to secure more men to work in auxiliary programs.

J. Auxiliaries can sometimes betray confidence; indeed, any employees can. Auxiliaries should be thoroughly oriented toward keeping all confidential matters within the confines of their teaching team.

Advantages of Auxiliaries in Schools

It is now pretty well established that teachers need help if they are to do all of the things required to individualize instruction. Following are some advantages of having auxiliaries in a school:

A. Every person is a unique resource of his own feelings and perceptions. This makes every human being a potential resource to the classroom teacher.

B. By the very nature of their responsibility, auxiliaries relate to children in a relaxed way. This sometimes gives them opportunities to develop rapport with children that busy teachers find difficult because of the complex set of tasks they are asked to accomplish.

C. Auxiliaries may relate to parents better than classroom teachers in some instances.

D. Auxiliaries in schools bring adults into very close relationships with each other. Children need to see adults planning, instructing, and evaluating instruction.

E. An auxiliary working in a very narrow area of the curriculum, such as sewing or mechanics, brings expertise into the school that cannot be found anywhere on the regular staff.

F. Auxiliaries can change the atmosphere of the school almost overnight by their attention to housekeeping, art projects, and bulletin boards.

G. Oftentimes school staffs are made up entirely of women. Bringing men into the school via the auxiliary program can be helpful to both boys and girls who may need a male model.

H. Auxiliaries working in schools force planning. The better teachers plan, the more children will learn.

Tasks Performed by Auxiliaries

The debate goes on about what is an appropriate role, or set of tasks for the auxiliary. It has never been resolved, and probably never will until educators realize that nearly anything they can do, some auxiliary can do better. Therefore, it is almost impossible to define the role or assign tasks, except in a very general way. At the risk of limiting the activities of auxiliaries, following are some examples of ways they might contribute to certain aspects of the school program:

Library Auxiliaries

Assist children with check in and out of books.
Teach library skills.
Repair books, magazines.
Keep the library neat in appearance by arranging books, putting up classroom book sharing projects, and supervising students who may be in charge of putting books on the shelves.
Helping students with research projects.
Work with the librarian in accessioning, requisitioning, and cataloging of books.
Work with classroom teachers to secure materials that complement a certain aspect of study.
Build free materials kits.
Go through old issues of newspapers and magazines and build instructional devices.
Keep vertical files and pamphlet files in order.
Take children to the city library, bookmobile and bookstores for book selection.

Audio Visual Auxiliaries

Check in and out of machines and materials.
Preview movies and filmstrips.
Order needed audio visual materials from central supply.
Duplicate materials using photocopies and thermofax machines.
Make transparencies.
Administer clerical tasks involving ordering, receiving, and cataloging of materials.
Keep inventory of audio visual equipment.
Hold in-service with staff members who may feel they need help with some of the machines.
Order free films and filmstrips.
Take pictures of school activities.
Repair audio visual machines.

Working Directly with Teachers

Correcting exercises and recording results.
Give spelling tests.
Record spelling tests on tape.
Build bulletin boards.

Obtain supplies from supply area.
Help teachers with housekeeping in their areas.
Help children with clothing.
Tutor one child.
Work with children in programmed instruction.
Supervise independent study.
Obtain pictures, or visual aids equipment including getting it ready before the lesson and operation during the lesson.
Obtain pictures, books, make charts, prepare classroom displays and enter information on the chalkboard as directed by the teacher.
Handle routine interruptions for the teacher like messages from other rooms, phone calls, and deliveries.
Float around the room and help students having trouble with assigned work.
Take care of opening exercises.
Small group reinforcement.
Take attendance.
Make-up work.
Pre-test, check-test, and post-test on learning packages.
Build classroom resource files.
Arrange speakers.
Prepare lessons for homebound students.
Tell stories.

Mathematics

Make audio tapes for reinforcement.
Filing, record keeping and testing in contract teaching.
Build mathematics games.
Small group work.

Science

Record observations.
Teach children the scientific method.
Make collections.
Accompany children on science field trips.
Help with laboratory work.
Secure resource persons.

Social Studies

Make maps.
Help children with projects.

Hold small group discussions.
Prepare for special holidays.

Language Arts

Work with children in spelling.
Take language experience dictation.
Make language experience books with children.
Help children select books.
Work with special students on needed skills.
Review difficult words.
Read to children.
Make a class newspaper.
Help students with written composition.
Story telling.
Book sharing.
Hold reading conferences with children.

Music

Build instruments with children.
Report on composers.
Play instruments for children.
Teach children about various instruments or how to play them.

General

Make-up work.
Collect money.
Attend meetings of parents, staff or students.
Inventory books and supplies.

Student Supervision

Supervise students in the halls.
Supervise students in intramural activities.
Supervise students confined to the classroom because of weather or illness.
Supervise hot lunch area.
Supervise students remaining at school for after school activities.
Supervise children on the playground.
Transport children to and from school who are ill.
Administer first aid.
Supervise bus students.

The list could go on and on. In an effective auxiliary program, there simply isn't anything that some auxiliary could not do as well as or better than the classroom teacher. The only rule to apply when using auxiliaries is: The only limiting factor is the ability of the classroom teacher to think creatively enough to assign an appropriate task, and the ability of the auxiliary to carry it out.

Checklist for Auxiliaries

How does an auxiliary know when the time is right for him to begin getting deeply involved in the school program? How does the auxiliary know when the time is right for him to begin working closely with children? The checklist that follows asks nineteen questions directly related to the instructional program and the readiness of the auxiliary for involvement in the program. When half or more of these questions can be answered affirmatively, the auxiliary is ready to work very closely with children.

Checklist For Auxiliaries

Question:	1	2	3	4	5	6	7	8	9	10	11	12	13	14	15	16	17	18	19
Yes																			
No																			
Partly																			

1. Do I have a plan for developing rapport with children?
2. Do I take note of the children's likes, dislikes, attitudes and interests?
3. Do I have rapport with the adults around me?
4. Do I take time to plan with my teachers?
5. Do I plan my lessons well?
6. Do I make myself helpful by offering my services to the teacher when I see that something needs to be done?
7. Do I give children choices?
8. Do I give individual help when I see that it is needed?
9. Do I know when to retreat from children and allow them to go it alone?
10. Do I observe closely the techniques employed by the classroom teacher, and follow-through with small groups?
11. Do I reinforce positive behavior of children?

12. Do I reflectively listen to those around me?
13. Do I take time to evaluate myself periodically?
14. Do I accept criticism and suggestions without getting upset?
15. Can I confront others when I am concerned about their behavior?
16. Do I carry out the classroom teacher's directions?
17. Do I give the classroom teacher adequate notice of my absence?
18. Do I avoid criticism of the children, teachers or school?
19. Do I know how to invite stable limits in children?

Figure 1-2

Tips on Working with Auxiliary Personnel

Remember that several hundred years of working as a *lone wolf* is not the best prerequisite for using auxiliaries. Constant efforts will need to be made to keep the program running smoothly. Following are some tips that might help make the program run smoothly:

Plan Together

When two or more people work together, they must plan together. Try to arrange special sessions when you can plan with your supportive staff. Planning for the use of teacher aides is usually scheduled during the school day. Scheduling for such auxiliaries as parents, students from colleges or universities, neighborhood youth corp students, or student tutors might, of necessity, be scheduled after school.

Including Auxiliaries in Your Plans

Rarely should a teacher or a teaching team work in isolation from their supportive staff. Notice of meetings, in-service workshops, administrative handouts, etc. should be made available to those who support your classroom program. Of course, good judgment should be used about whether or not to invite a student tutor to a teacher workshop. However, if the student were a high school student belonging to Future Teachers of America, it might be very appropriate to ask him to attend the meeting, especially if the meeting were on mathematics and he happened to be working with a group of students needing help in a certain area of mathematics.

Decision Making

Whenever possible, try to include auxiliaries in the decision making process. Failure to do so will again reinforce the fact that people on the low end of the hierarchy do not count. At times, when the auxiliary plays only a minor role in a given task, there will probably be little or no role in the decision making process. However, if the task is to be carried out by the auxiliary, they should have a great deal of voice in the decisions affecting that task.

Social Relationships

For the best possible rapport to exist among adults working in a team relationship, efforts need to be made to meet outside of the classroom. These social gatherings can do much to cement relationships. Be sure to include supportive staff as well as the regular professional staff.

Exposure

Supportive staff should not be expected to work in isolation. Give them opportunities to grow like any other members of the team. When school visitations are scheduled, ask teacher aides, volunteer parents, and student tutors to participate. The trip to and from the visit might be as productive as the visit itself.

Keeping the Focus on Instruction

There are almost as many differences in ability, creativity, and interest among auxiliaries as there are among teachers. The professionals in a school need to be aware of this. If not, there is a chance that very well-trained, highly creative auxiliaries may be spending a great deal of their time doing the very things you have worked so hard to keep teachers from doing.

Look at every task and try to find the most appropriate person to do it. Avoid at all costs having any member of the auxiliary staff doing something over a long period of time that is far below their level of competency. For instance, a teacher aide who has a masters degree in art should not be spending all of her time cutting letters for bulletin boards.

One way to keep the focus on instruction is to ask auxiliaries to keep logs of their activities. This will give you a ready reference to how they are spending their time and how well teachers are planning for their utilization.

Separate their tasks into three categories: 1. Instruction 2. Building Instructional Materials 3. Clerical. Consider both one and two as very appropriate for keeping the focus on instruction. Too much emphasis on number three, especially by well-trained auxiliaries, will no doubt affect the total effectiveness of the program.

Following is a sample auxiliary log and how a teacher aide used her time over a period of nearly three months. The teacher aide was an instructional aide who had about two years of college and had taught in the elementary school.

Primary Teacher Aide Log

<u>Key</u>

I—Instruction
IM—Instructional Materials
C—Clerical

September 25-29

(I) Checked Primary I comprehension of beginning reading skills. Their progress is being recorded in individual folders. I helped the teacher bring these up to date. Began working with six Primary I students on alphabet recognition. This group has extremely short attention span and needs a variety of activities. We are presently matching letter to like sounds and pictures, using an alphabet flashboard game and working through a readiness workbook.

(I) Read with a Primary II student who lacks knowledge of basic sight words. He is an intelligent boy, but very much behind in reading. We are reading in a 1^2 book, making a list of problem words and concentrating on initial and ending sounds.

(I) Worked with a Primary II student on beginning consonant blends. They're especially confused on ch, sh, wh, and th. Have been meeting with the same children at math time since they have difficulty with the tens and ones concept.

(C) Cut letters and put up pupil's art work for a Primary III wall display.

(C) Typed and ran off copies of a test and several seat work sheets.

(I) Corrected math center work in Primary I and conferred with children about mistakes.

(I) Read stories to kindergarten children.

October 2-6

(C) Filled in general information on children's individual records. Figured ages in years and months.

(C) Graded some Primary III tests and scored the results.

(I) Began helping a Primary II student with handwriting problems. He cannot remember on which lines to begin and end letters.

(C) Mounted pictures for Primary I. Mounted pictures of common objects on 3x5 cards. The word will later go on the card and all cards will be placed in a word recognition file.

(I) Took dictation, from Primary I children. They were to find interesting pictures in magazines and create sentences about the picture. I wrote their sentences on paper and then the children read them back to me. We then made and titled booklets.

(I) Began working with a readiness group on letter recognition.

(C) Corrected and filed seat work papers in Primary II.

(I) Gave and scored a Primary III *Weekly Reader* test.

(I) Took two classes to the library.

October 9-13

(I) Began reading with two boys each morning instead of just the Primary II child. Two teachers found that they each had a child with the same reading difficulty. The two boys get along well together. Rusty is quite shy and is slowly being drawn out of his shell. Larry is showing new interest in reading. They love to compete for flash cards. Each morning we have a contest to see who remembers the most sight words. Usually they tie.

(C) Mixed paint for a Primary II afternoon art class.

(C) Made name cards for Primary III book report file.

(I) Worked with small groups of Primary III students having difficulty with telling time. They all had individual clock faces and practiced times which I dictated.

(I) Worked with individual kindergartners on the fine art of tying shoes.

(C) Typed poems for the Primary II class. They are presently reading and illustrating poetry.

(C) Sharpened sixty pencils for the kindergarten class.

(I) Organized some games on the playground this week. Some of the children who don't go home for lunch need supervised activity. They all seemed to enjoy it.

October 16-20

(I) Began working with groups of five to seven Primary I students on various levels of the Dolch basic vocabulary list. This will be a continuous project. We are stressing a game atmosphere with these words. A few members of the class are not ready for word recognition and I am still working with them on the alphabet.

(IM) Previewed a film for a Primary I class. Told the teacher what the story involved and described the main character.

(I) I have been working with small groups of a Primary II class on the tens and ones concept. Now they are learning about hundreds. Two afternoons I took some of the children into the hallway to give them some extra practice. Two afternoons the teacher took half of the class into the hallway while I worked with half in the room. We changed sections each day. The breakdown of size seemed to be very helpful.

October 23-28

(I) Read a science test to two boys who are far below grade level in reading. They were unable to work the test in class, but both did average work when it was read to them.

(C) Tallied up book club money and orders for Primary I and Primary II classes.

(I) Worked with small groups of kindergarten students on shape and color concepts.

(I) Administered two Primary I reading tests. They were given individually since both children are ahead of their classes.

(IM) Began working on sight word packets for Primary II. This involves a series of packets on three levels. There are from 30-50 cards in each packet.

October 30-November 3

(IM) Typed large catalog cards for Primary III unit on how to find a book in the library. Did a duplicate set for the other Primary III class.

(I) Worked with kindergarten group on concepts of more and fewer. We drew sets of objects on large newsprint. They were to make sets with more or fewer than mine.

(C) Typed up stories Primary II students had written and put them into a booklet.

November 6-10

(I) Took a Primary I class from 9:00-10:45 while the teacher was giving a teaching demonstration. Had an art lesson, read a story, and had a gym class.

(IM) Made two word games for Primary I. Each is on a sheet of tag board. One is a winding stream with stones across it. The object is to put a word on each stone and have the children read themselves across the stream. Anyone who cannot do it falls in and gets wet. The other game is a ladder. It works the same way with a word on each rung. Children try to climb the ladder.

(IM) Had time this week to work on the word packets for Primary I. Got two complete sets done. The children can read through the packets independently for word practice. I am in the process now of checking one reading group on their recognition of all the words. Their progress is recorded in their individual folders.

(C) Ran off dittos for science and math centers. These are for a Primary I class. Also ran off language arts papers. These were stapled together into individual booklets to be handed to each child on that level.

(IM) Checked some Primary I writing papers. Made up new practice writing papers for those children having difficulty. Each child practices on the letters which he finds hard to make correctly. The papers are placed in the writing center in the room.

November 13-17

(C) Blew up a Thanksgiving turkey with the opaque projector. Then painted it for Primary I. The teacher gave me two other animals to paint sometime in the future.

(I) Took a morning kindergarten class while the teacher attended a lecture. We did the routine things plus papers on the more and fewer concept and the meaning of sequence.

November 20-22

(IM) Typed work sheets and keys for individualized math program. These sheets will go into a Primary III math center.

(IM) Compiled booklet of handwriting do's and don'ts for a Primary III class.

(I) Took a Primary II class for an hour and a half while the teacher met with parents to discuss individualized reading.

(I) Began having conferences with Primary II students on books they have read. As a part of the individualized program, the children talk about their books to the teacher and then plan a way to share them with the class. Their books, descriptions, and problem words are recorded on individual conference sheets.

November 27-December 1

(I) Worked with two Primary I art groups. The children were doing murals as a finish-up activity for a unit on the four seasons. There were four groups, each of which chose a leader and created one of the seasons. The teacher and I circulated, making sure that each group remembered to include all the things they had discussed in class.

(I) Began working with a Primary III accelerated math group. There are six children who are working through the math book at their own rate of speed. Of course, they need supervision. They meet at the regular math time and I am there to answer questions and explain confusing concepts.

(I) Assisted a Primary III teacher two afternoons with a weaving project. Children were making place mats from large sheets of woven construction paper.

December 4-8

(C) Cut paper for a kindergarten Christmas gift project, a Primary I tree decoration and another Primary I art project.

(C) Cut collars and bows for Primary II to wear in their Christmas program.

(I) Began reading with a Primary III student who is very disinterested in reading of any sort. He is not lacking in ability, he simply doesn't enjoy it. Since his main interest is sports, we've started a paperback sports story. We are hoping a high interest level story will motivate him to try others.[7]

---

[7]Jerry L. Abbott, "Teacher Aide Progress Report: Keeping the Focus on Instruction," (Progress Report of the Teacher and His Staff Project, Grand Forks Public Schools, 1968), pp. 10-14.

During the period from September 25th until December 8th, it was found the teacher aide spent approximately 85 per cent of her time either carrying out an instructional task or building instructional materials. Only 15 per cent of the time was spent doing clerical tasks.

There are other ways of refining the use of the teacher aide log. You could add the dimension of time spent in a task to the log for an even clearer picture of how the auxiliary spent her time. You could also apply the log to one teacher or one teaching team to see how they utilized the auxiliary.

Periodically it is well to look closely at the members of the auxiliary program and find out how well they are being utilized. It will reinforce the implementation of the model for auxiliaries, as well as apply some pressure to look closely at role.

Auxiliary Training

Any school which makes a commitment to the use of auxiliaries must make a commitment to on-going pre-service and in-service education for them. Although the purpose of this discussion is not to structure a workshop for such in-service, following are some of the principles that should be thoroughly covered:

Learning Theory
Principles of growth and development
Competencies in the various academic disciplines
Human relations skills
Skills in handling misbehavior
Clerical skills such as office machines, filing and correcting
School philosophy
Policies and regulations
Trends in education (open education, alternative schools, technology in education)
Accountability
Stable limits for staff (dress, speech, punctuality, etc.)
Functions of auxiliaries
Audio Visual
Library
Special services

No two workshops will be alike, as all schools will have special needs. However, when setting up a workshop for auxiliaries, it might be well to include most of the above and possibly structure the workshop around the following process:

A. What are the skills that auxiliaries should have?

B. What are the stated behavioral objectives for each skill?

C. What kind of terminal behavior should result?

D. Evaluation

Sample Set of Objectives for an
Auxiliary Workshop

Once it is decided what you want auxiliaries to know, try to write very specific objectives for each skill. Below is a sample set of objectives that might be helpful when structuring a workshop for auxiliaries.

The participant will:

A. State in written form ten reasons for promoting a more extensive usage of auxiliaries.

B. Distinguish with a written paragraph the basic distinction between the use of teacher aides in a self-contained school and one which uses differentiated staffing.

C. Select five research-based guidelines for the selection of teacher aides.

D. List five kinds of auxiliary help available in his community for next school year.

E. Diagram an organizational chart for the functioning of an auxiliary program in his school setting.

F. List ten steps which could be taken to initiate a program of community involvement in his school district.

G. Identify ten characteristics of his school which justify the employment of teacher aides.

H. Suggest, by writing three paragraphs, how the concepts of modern educational practice and an auxiliary program might be employed to reach the program goals of his school.

I. Develop a research design for an auxiliary program in his school district. Include the following: Identification of needs, Implementation model, Evaluation model.

J. Demonstrate a knowledge of the auxiliary selection tasks by listing at least six general qualities of successful auxiliaries.

K. List at least three sources of teacher aides in a community.

L. Formulate statements explaining two important points to stress during interviewing of auxiliaries.

M. Identify by written statements those persons who should be involved in the interview and selection task.

N. By reading sample booklets and surveying his own school system, be prepared to develop a booklet or set of instructions for your auxiliaries and teachers.

O. Demonstrate a knowledge of appropriate ways to prepare a staff for the introduction of auxiliaries to your school system by making a brief time-table outline of projected activities.

P. Prepare a list of at least twenty-five ways auxiliaries might assist teachers.

Q. Identify by written statements at least two ways teacher aides might be assigned in your school.

R. List at least five schools a staff might visit in preparation for the introduction of an auxiliary program.

S. Demonstrate a knowledge of the development of a pre-service workshop by making a rough design of such things as: curriculum content, length of time for workshop, and basic costs.

T. Demonstrate a knowledge of the development and role of an in-service workshop by making a time-table for the number of workshops and a rough design for each. Include such things as: curriculum content, dates and length of time and basic costs.

U. Identify by written statements and in order of importance to your system at least three central topics for stress in such a workshop series.[8]

What Does Research Say?

For three years, the Grand Forks Public Schools was part of a Federally funded Title III project on the use of teacher aides in three selected schools. The formal research includes the use of several well-known instruments. The informal part of the research includes the comments of parents, students, teacher aides, teachers and administrators.

Formal Research

At the end of each year of the project, an extensive evaluation report was prepared for dissemination. Following is a summary of

---

[8]Jerry L. Abbott, Margaret Abbott, and Harold Bergquist, "Organization of a Teacher Aide Training Program," (Behavioral Objectives for a Teacher Aide Training Program, Grand Forks, North Dakota, 1970), pp. 1-3.

the three years of research by Dr. John Thompson, former Director of Graduate Studies in Education at the University of North Dakota.

Evaluation Implications: Teacher and His Staff

The research component of the implementation of the "Teacher and His Staff" concept was concerned with attempting to evaluate the function of aides as agents for change in the schools in which they worked. Aides were, in a sense, an unknown quantity in the education structure of the schools of North Dakota.

Project Year One

The rationale for the first year evaluation was to identify control groups who were not utilizing aides in their building, and to compare them on several dimensions, over time, with the teachers and pupils who were in the experimental schools. An initial administration of the evaluation instruments was made in October, and baseline comparisons between the groups were made. A second administration to the same groups was made in April, after the experimental group had been working with aides for several months.

Several of the instruments were designed to test the effect of aides on the attitudes of teachers with whom they worked. There were no significant differences between the control and experimental groups in the fall administration. However, by spring, the teachers in the schools in which aides were used had significantly higher opinions about the value of aides. Those teachers were prone to express a willingness to assign aides to a wide range of tasks which both the experimental and control groups had previously shunned.

Teachers' rapport with students, in rooms where aides were used, remained constant throughout the year, while in the control schools the mean rapport scores measured by a standardized rating scale (The Minnesota Teacher Attitude Inventory) had dropped by the end of the year.

The question of possible change in the academic achievement level of children who had the benefit of aides in the classroom was examined. Large group samplings of changes in the ITBS did not produce the expected difference in achievement levels between the experimental and control student groups. It would appear that testing large groups of students, many of whom had little exposure to teacher aides, is an inappropriate way to determine academic differences.

Project Years Two and Three

The evaluation during the initial project year was a comparison of control and experimental groups, while the second year focused on the experimental group only. The thrust of the measurement was to determine if change was linear over time or whether it was, in effect, one dimensional in nature. A special effort was made to compare beginning teachers, who were in the experimental schools for the first time, against the change pattern of those who were more experienced in the use of aides.

Although there were exceptions among the various tests, it appeared that change in attitude about the value and the usage of aides did not have a linear characteristic. Teachers who were experienced in using aides did not make better use of aides in the second year than in the first year. New teachers were tested before they began work in the fall and their scores were not significantly different from the pre-tests of the experimental and control teachers from previous years. Their scores at the end of the year were not significantly different from the teachers who were finishing their second year working with aides. The success of an aide program appears to be determined during the initial year. Teachers did not change significantly after that time.

The researchers were unwilling to accept *ipso facto* the tenet that aides are economically valuable to a school district. A cost/utility study was initiated and continued for one year. During that year only six of the fourteen aides who were involved achieved a positive cost-to-utility ratio. Feedback of this information to the district had important effects for the type of use aides were assigned in the second year, as well as for adjusting the salary scale of the aides in the district.

These adjustments had a dramatic affect on aide usage during the second year of the cost study. During that year all but three of the fourteen aides had a positive cost/utility ratio.

The fact that aides cost less to hire than teachers does not necessarily mean they are a saving to the district. The study shows that their economic value to the district is determined by the utility of the tasks which they perform. The key component in the change between the first and second year was in the amount and percentage of time aides worked at tasks labeled instructional in nature. Assigning utility values to tasks may have an additional value for school districts. Use of a panel of board members, teachers on the negotiation team, and administrators has the effect of involving many people to establish objectives for programs in the district. Sharing these decision making chores may have a positive effect on teachers as well as board members.

An interview schedule conducted on a sample of parents whose children were in schools employing aides revealed some interesting findings. Parents knew about the jobs aides performed. Many believed that aides had been a positive influence upon their own children, and they were enthusiastic supporters of the aide program. From a public relations point of view, the aide project was a success. In an era when schools are "under fire" on many issues, an aide program may be a valuable adjunct to the organizational pattern of a system.

Near the end of the project, teachers and aides were asked to scale a long list of pre-scaled questions about the functions of the aides. Ranking mean scores and using correlation techniques to interpret the data revealed a high degree of agreement among the groups about the tasks which aides "do" as well as "ought to do." In Grand Forks, the perceptions of both aides and teachers on the position of the aide are highly congruent, obviously a highly desirable finding in any complex organization.

Training aides is an expensive undertaking, particularly if an aide is unhappy or unsuccessful in her work. Clearly, it would be an advantage to an employing school district to have a set of criteria which would correlate with aide success.

An exploratory study to attempt to arrive at predictive criteria was undertaken. Prior to their employment, aides were given a battery of tests and inventories; in addition, personal data was recorded. Teachers with whom aides worked made multiple ratings of the effectiveness of the aides during the year. These were compared to the data previously collected. Certain sub-scales of the 16 Personality Factor Inventory appeared to highly correlate with aide success (as rated by the teachers). The desired qualities on the inventory were: (A) reserved, detached, cool; (E) humble, mild, accommodating; (Q2) group dependent, a joiner and a follower; and (Q4) tranquil, torpid, and unfrustrated. The preliminary finding was that prospective aides whose scores on the inventory are toward the end of the continuum described by the words listed above would be rated highly by teachers. Of course, it will be necessary to continue the study over time to determine the actual predictive value of this inventory in hiring aides.

This report is an effort to summarize certain aspects of the "Teacher and His Staff" project which appear to be significant as well as having potential for further study. Complete research data is available by contacting the nearest ERIC center.[9]

Informal Research

Following is a summary of comments made by teachers, parents, administrators, students and teacher aides during the three years of the Teacher and His Staff project.

Teacher Aides

Each teacher has her own way of using a teacher aide. Some are very good at using us in an instructional way and some use us mostly for clerical things.

Working with children in tutorial ways, small groups, or playing with them in the playground is very advantageous because the situation is so intimate.

Today I was working with a group of boys in *Reader's Digest Skill Builders.* One boy said, "Oh, I'm so happy I can read this." It made me feel very good.

I feel I have an exceptional group of teachers to assist. Some are more organized than others. One teacher has a way of expressing her appreciation that really adds "zip" to my day. As I was leaving her room today she handed me a note which read, "Thank you . . . the lesson went so well today . . . the kids were interested and attentive."

The worst experience I have ever had as a teacher aide occurred to me this month. During my supervision of the lunch line a primary teacher interrupted me and took over the discipline of an intermediate child. I was sure her intentions were good. I feel it affected my relationship with the students. I was pretty upset.

[9]Margaret Abbott and John Thompson, *Implementation of the Teacher and His Staff Concept: Research Effort* (Grand Forks, North Dakota, 1970), pp. 39-42.

I am spending more time conferencing with students in mathematics and reading. I like this. It keeps me from being the "dumb kids' teacher."

Students

I get more individual attention with more adults in the room.

When the teacher says, "look it up," the teacher aide is there to help you.

Teachers are so busy. Teacher aides are more free to answer questions.

We have two men in our room. It is nice to talk to another girl about some things.

I like the way they are used. It helps the teacher individualize.

I think teachers are fresher in the afternoon when they don't have to chase kids in the playground during the noon hour.

We need more than one teacher when we do so much group work and conferencing.

Sometimes the teacher aide can explain things better.

Yesterday the tape got all funny and she fixed it.

If you get hurt on the playground the teacher aide will help you fix it.

I think they are very helpful. They help groups get organized and help individual people having trouble. They also watch the lunch line so there are no fights.

Parents

I think the teacher aide program is very worthwhile and successful. Any child that needs personal attention can get it, while the rest of the class is not held back. The teacher can concentrate on the main job of teaching and is freed from the administrative details and tasks which do not require the teacher's experience and qualifications.

With six children attending the schools I can truly state my gratitude and my admiration for what these dedicated people are achieving.

The aide is quite often and literally the "spoonful of sugar" that helps the "medicine go down."

There is a definite need for teacher aides in the schools. The aide provides a personal relationship to the student on a one-to-one basis. Conferences are held often to check progress, collect papers, and help solve any problems. In order for the students to want to strive ahead, they need this special personal close relationship.

Because of this growth in education, the teacher today is charged with greater responsibility toward her students, in that she must possess more extensive knowledge, plan more challenging lessons, and be widely versed in the problems young people have, growing up in today's complex society.

This assistance is of great value to the teacher in that her energies are channeled into the evaluation of the student as well as being able to evaluate her own teaching methods.

From the student standpoint, I believe, comes the greatest value. Children are exposed to several usually responsive, relaxed adults with whom they may feel more readily at ease to relate any problems they may have. Students need the contact of more than one person.

As a parent I am most pleased with the warmth and concern of the aide who has been associated with my child. She has been a marked asset in his class as she relates so well with the children and has provided a positive influence on them. This enhances their educational growth as it affects their attitudes toward school, authority figures, and themselves.

Teachers

Our teacher aide has proven to be an invaluable asset in our attempt to individualize instruction. She is utilized in many ways, some of which are: typing dittos, correcting papers, constructing charts and graphs, supervising small groups, and conducting individual conferences.

My language experience program has improved 100 per cent since I have the services of a teacher aide. She takes dictation, finds materials for the children, and makes booklets of their writings.

The love and kindness my aide shows these young children is very important, for they "aim to please" if they know "you care."

My teacher aide has helped in more ways than can be expressed. I've never asked her for assistance and been told she is too busy. My days are so much smoother now.

Your room cannot be a "sacred portal" if you expect to work with aides. I never want to teach in a school without teacher aides. What a wonderful learning atmosphere we have developed as a result of not being bogged down with clerical tasks.[10]

Administration

The important task is to get good people and help teachers utilize them to the utmost.

A constant in-service program is necessary for maximum utilization.

The only limitation in the use of the aides is their ability and the ability of the classroom teacher to use them in a creative way.

Human relations is the biggest problem facing us in the utilization of teacher aides.

Relieving teachers of supervisory duties is no small matter. It is inhuman to ask a teacher to chase kids all noon hour and then expect good performance during the afternoon.

I notice quite a difference in the attractiveness of the rooms. The aides do many creative projects that help develop classroom atmosphere.

I am thankful for the teacher aides in my building because they help me do a better job. The noon hour is one of the only times during the day that I can conference with teachers. This was never possible in the days when I supervised the lunchroom and halls.[11]

Summary

Hopefully it has been established that auxiliaries are imperatives in all schools. They are the first step to ACTION. The instructional program simply cannot get off the ground until it is firmly undergirded with a strong auxiliary program.

And it isn't enough that each school have a program—it must be a good one. It must not be the kind of program that divides up the staff by some convenient number and employs some teacher aides to "cover the ground." In fact, blanketing the school with teacher aides who do no more than bounce from one teacher to the next

---

[10]Margaret Abbott, *Progress Report: Implementation of the Teacher and His Staff Concept* (Grand Forks, North Dakota, 1969), pp. 13-28.

[11]Margaret Abbott, *Application for Continuation Grant: Implementation of the Teacher and His Staff Concept* (Grand Forks, North Dakota, 1969), pp. 51-55.

will do little to affect instructional improvement. Only when they are part of a well defined auxiliary program will their influence be deeply felt.

So once more there is a call to lead. Someone, namely the building principal, must develop, in cooperation with his staff, a model for an auxiliary program and work constantly to improve that model. Only then will things begin to happen.

Auxiliary IDEA Bank

This chapter has given the reader ideas on how to organize and implement an auxiliary program. The Auxiliary IDEA Bank is a series of questions which attempt to make the reader even more cognizant of the dynamics of having auxiliaries in schools. The short responses following each question should further promote thought and discussion about auxiliaries.

A. What should auxiliaries do in schools?

    Ans: Anything you can do can probably be done equally as well by some auxiliary.

B. What things must auxiliaries not do in schools?

    Ans: Always remember that teachers have been charged with the main responsibility of diagnosis and prescription. Talented as auxiliaries may be, they support and supplement instruction, and never should be allowed to carry it out alone.

C. How can auxiliaries be made to feel as though they belong?

    Ans: Not long ago I participated in a day-long workshop on teacher aides. My group discussed aide problems. The consensus of this group was that all problems fall into two categories: planning and stroking.

D. How can we involve auxiliaries socially?

    Ans: Let your imagination be your guide.

E. How can you meaningfully plan with auxiliaries when they are not an on-going part of a teaching team?

    Ans: It isn't easy. Set aside some time before school, during the noon break, or after school. Try to find technological devices that can at times free you to plan for instruction during the school day.

F. Should teacher aides be part of a team, or is it best to schedule them with several teachers in self-contained rooms?

Ans: In my experience, assigning teacher aides to teams on a permanent basis has been far superior to scheduling them into several self-contained rooms. You may have to use this type of scheduling if your school is not organized for team teaching. Beware, else these aides become the *dumb kids' teachers.*

G. Do we need to be concerned about state and local laws that govern auxiliaries?

Ans: Yes. Always try to work within the limits of the law. The key is to know why you do something. Courts, I am confident, will judge you well if what you do is both prudent and reasonable.

H. How can we evaluate the contributions made by auxiliaries?

Ans: There are many instruments available to determine success (see ERIC Abstracts). Be sure your design doesn't call for the aides to work with selected students and then test large numbers of students. Don't forget to sample the perceptions of teachers, students and parents.

I. Should teacher aides come out of the regular staffing ratio or should they be extra staff?

Ans: Recent graphs comparing the expenditure curve with the total numbers of students in schools indicate that we should no longer try to improve education by the process of additional monies alone. I feel paid auxiliaries should come out of the regular staffing ratio, when possible, with the saved money being diverted to things other than people costs.

J. Should auxiliaries who are as well-trained as teachers be used in the same way?

Ans: Although every effort should be made to capitalize upon the competencies of auxiliary personnel, it is both unethical and illegal to use auxiliaries as certified teachers.

K. Should auxiliaries who are paid have fringe benefits? Which ones?

Ans: I feel auxiliaries should have the same fringe benefits that are now provided for certified teachers.

L. What are the teacher's responsibilities to auxiliaries?

Ans: Planning and stroking.

M. How can we help auxiliaries gain new skills on the job?

Ans: If the in-service program of the school or team is exciting, auxiliaries will learn new skills at a rapid rate.

N. How do you handle the situation when an auxiliary has greater skill in a particular subject than the classroom teacher?

Ans: Just stand out of their light. These are times when you become their auxiliary.

O. How do we keep auxiliaries from being the person who teaches all of the slow children?

Ans: This is probably the number one problem to avoid when working with auxiliaries, especially paid teacher aides. Sound, on-going planning can avoid this problem.

P. How do we give auxiliaries positive feedback about what they are doing in school?

Ans: Reports on their activities, Good News Letters, reinforcement during planning sessions, non-verbal communication, and co-planning with them in such a way that they meet success most of the time when working with children.

Q. How can we best help auxiliaries who are responsible for student supervision?

Ans: Help them develop new skills such as reflective listening, congruent sending, setting stable limits and problem solving. And leave them alone when they are confronting a child about his misbehavior, unless they ask for your assistance.

R. How can we unlock the creativity of auxiliaries so they can meaningfully contribute to the classroom?

Ans: Involve them in success experiences as often as possible and help them develop new skills which better help them meet the needs of children.

S. How can paid auxiliaries help to spread specialists over a greater area so as to affect more children?

Ans: This is unique to each school. Ask the staff for their input, keeping in mind that teacher aides cannot be given total responsibility for classroom instruction.

T. Can the untrained auxiliary be used in the classroom?

Ans: Absolutely. This is what the book is all about.

U. Are we making use of all the auxiliary help that is available to us?

Ans: The help we are now receiving from auxiliaries is the *tip of the iceberg.*

V. What plans do we have for an on-going program of training for auxiliaries?

Ans: You must ask yourself this question often.

W. How do we handle conflict between auxiliaries and the professional staff?

Ans: It is true that when people are brought into close relationships with each other, as they almost always are in any innovative endeavor, conflict is sure to result. Every staff should be involved in human development programs that help staff members find the entwining relationship with each other.

Following are examples of human development programs that can help you find this new relationship:

Bessell, Harold and Uvaldo Palomares, *Human Development Program* (San Diego, Calif., Human Development Training Institute, 1969).

Borton, Terry, *Reach, Touch and Teach* (New York, N.Y., McGraw-Hill Book Company, 1970).

Glasser, William, *Schools Without Failure* (Los Angeles, Calif., Educator Training Center, 1969).

Gordon, Thomas, *Parent Effectiveness Training* (Pasadena, Calif., Effectiveness Training Associates, 1971).

Randolph, Norma, William Howe and Elizabeth Achterman, *Self Enhancing Education* (Santa Clara, Calif., Self Enhancing Education, Inc., 1972).

Chapter 2

Tutor Assisted Instruction (TAI)

The announcement by the National Reading Council that 10,000,000 tutors would be needed by 1980 is some indication of the faith that educators are now placing in auxiliary personnel, especially parents and their children.

So many things have been tried, all with varying degrees of success. The latest development, that of enlisting the help of auxiliary personnel in the education of children, is no doubt going to make significant impact upon American education.

Tutors have been used in schools from the very beginning. The early one-room school with its thirty, and oftentimes more, children and one teacher used tutors out of necessity. It was commonplace for older children to teach younger ones.

When the schools began to reorganize into larger units, everything from the room the children sat in to the curriculum they studied began to be compartmentalized, and the use of tutors declined. Now, because of the advent of individualized instruction and the deep concern for humaneness in the schools, the use of tutors is on the increase.

There are many good reasons for implementing a tutor program. They are:

A. Students develop better work habits.
B. Students become more responsible.
C. Students are able to practice better self-management.
D. The underachieving student is receiving additional help.
E. Gifted children receive enrichment.
F. Students can pursue things that interest them.
G. Students are motivated to do a better job in school.
H. Self concept is strengthened through the one-to-one relationship.

For too long teachers have tried to go it alone. Rapid changes in the culture, technological advances in education, and a growing concern about the worth and uniqueness of all students makes it imperative that teachers seek help. And nowhere is it as plentiful than in the school itself.

One of the interesting things that has happened as a result of tutor programs is the realization that they are as beneficial to the tutor as they are to the tutee. In fact, many school districts are now using underachieving tutors with underachieving tutees and finding they both make significant gains in achievement.[1]

Never has there been a greater need to develop warm, loving and caring relationships between people. A culture as complex and transient as ours can create chasms between people. The implementation of humane programs in schools has the potential to build the bridges necessary to secure and maintain the entwining relationship.

Can Tutors Teach?

This is the question most often asked not only about tutors, but all other auxiliary personnel. How can untrained people teach? The answer can be found in something most teachers have encountered at one time or another. Have you ever tried to learn something and found that full meaning could not be grasped until you had taught it to someone else? And who is to say that teachers' colleges prepare one to be an expert in everything? Is it not entirely possible for a young boy or girl to have more information on a given subject than any teacher in the building?

---

[1] *Supervisors Manual: Youth Tutoring Youth* (New York, N.Y.: National Commission on Resources for Youth, Inc., 1968), p. 2.

And what about motivation? If someone is highly interested in something, he will be able to do things, he never thought possible.

Of course tutors cannot do it alone. They need the constant help and support of the classroom teacher. Rarely will the tutor be working in isolation, for only when the teacher and the tutor work closely will the impact of the program be deeply felt.

Self Concept

The relationship between how one views himself and his achievement in school is well known. The teacher, oftentimes, is not able to devote the time necessary for the strengthening of self. Some students come to her so lacking in self concept that only massive amounts of work will produce any results. So the teacher does the best she can, and devotes the major part of her time to cognitive development.

After viewing the work of hundreds of auxiliaries in schools you cannot help but be impressed by the role they play in the development of self. The teacher, because of her many responsibilities, has a steady pressure to keep things going in the classroom. Students pick up these strong non-verbal signals about their teachers' priorities and repress many of their feelings, which eventually affects their work in school and their view of self.

But if a classroom is lucky enough to have tutors or some other form of auxiliary help, there is often an inclination on the part of some students to develop a positive relationship with them. They do this because the auxiliary is in a far more relaxed role in the classroom, and therefore much more receptive to hearing feelings.

Watch the auxiliaries as they work with children. See the warm relationship that is built when a student aide from the university works with children in a small group, and watch a group of children the last day a student teacher is in the classroom. You cannot help but be impressed by the relationship that has been built.

Involvement Leads to Commitment

The link between involvement and commitment is also well known. To ask a person to change his behavior without first becoming involved with him is to ask for the impossible.

Dr. William Glasser, author of *Reality Therapy*, explains the relationship. He says that people have problems because they are unable to fulfill their needs.[2] How do you fulfill someone's needs? First you must get deeply involved with that person in a meaningful way. Only then will commitment for change result.

Dr. Glasser tells of working with a patient in a sanitarium who was completely immobilized. In a period of three months, this ninety-five-year-old man, who was completely helpless, became an active, vigorous, and self-sufficient member of the sanitarium. His senility was simply due to his reaction to isolation and noninvolvement. When he became involved with another human who was interested in him as a person, he found reason to change his behavior.

Needs, Dr. Glasser feels, can all be summarized into two basic areas: the need to love and be loved, and the need to feel we are worthwhile to ourselves and to others.[3] Only then will we find the ultimate satisfaction in life.

This can be further illustrated by an experiment that was done with animals several years ago. Two groups of rats were placed into a maze with a container of water at the end. The first group of rats worked their way through the maze and were allowed to fall into the water. It was observed that they swam around for one hour before drowning. The second group was then placed into the maze, allowed to fall into the water, but after a short time were taken out, dried off, talked to, and stroked. They were once again placed into the maze. It was observed that they swam around for fifty-four hours before drowning.

Living things respond when they know someone cares. Commitment for changed behavior will come only when human beings are able to find deep, personal, and meaningful ways to become involved with each other. Tutor programs can do just that.

Matching the Tutor and Tutee

The most common arrangement for matching tutors with their tutees is that of using intermediate children as tutors and primary children as tutees. Although a three-year age spread is generally a

---

[2]William Glasser, *Reality Therapy* (New York, N.Y.: Harper and Row Publishers, Inc., 1965), p. 5.

[3]Glasser, *Reality Therapy*, p. 9.

good rule, it need not always be the case. In our experience we have found that the three-year age difference can be violated if the tutor has some skill in the subject he is teaching. If he is not particularly knowledgeable in what he is doing, it could do serious damage to his self-image if the three-year age spread is violated.

Should boys be matched with boys and girls with girls? Although this might seem to be a logical way to match students, our experience with elementary age children has been that when the matching is done according to needs, interests, and abilities, there are as many boys who work with girls and girls who work with boys as members of the same sex working together.

Almost every conceivable arrangement for matching tutor with tutee can be found in the literature. Among the most common are:

> Parents tutoring infants or elementary children
> Lay professionals tutoring disadvantaged mothers and/or their children
> Upper elementary children tutoring primary children
> Disadvantaged junior or senior high students tutoring elementary children
> Gifted junior or senior high students tutoring elementary age children or each other
> College students tutoring elementary, secondary or each other
> Lay professionals like clergymen tutoring all levels of students
> Neighborhood Youth Corp or Volunteers in Service to America tutoring students of all levels
> Machines tutoring students of all levels
> Retired people tutoring students, usually elementary
> One culture of people tutoring another
> Educable mentally handicapped tutoring trainable mentally handicapped

Before deciding the combination of tutor to tutee, it is well to first decide the goals of the program. If a Big Brother-type relationship is the kind desired, consider using college students or some lay group that may be able to give the program a small amount of their time. However, if the problem is one of under-achievement and low self-image with a group of primary children, you might want to seek help from the students in your school, or some that could come on a regular basis and be involved in training programs.

Problems with Tutor Programs

Any change in the educational program is accompanied by problems as well as advantages. Tutor programs are no exception. Following are some of the more common concerns that will require considerable amounts of thought on the part of those in charge of the program:

Planning

One of the greatest problems of tutor programs is the tendency to match tutor with tutee and leave them alone. To do this is to so dilute the program that it will slowly disintegrate until it disappears. Any organizational plan that is chosen must be accompanied by close supervision on the part of the professional staff with weekly, if not daily, planning.

Goals Program Conflict

One of the greatest mistakes that can be made is to have a conflict between the stated goals of the program and the plan of operation. For instance, if the goal is to help zero in on problems of low self-image with severely disadvantaged children, don't adopt a program that calls for meeting children on an incidental basis in groups. You would want to select those who could best relate to this kind of child, and fashion a program that calls for regular one-to-one contact.

In Service Training

The one component that keeps running through all of the literature on the subject of tutoring is that of constant attention to training. The problems most often dealt with, such as low self-image, deficiencies in language and mathematics skills are not the kind of problems that can be dealt with by people who have no training. So the professional staff must pay constant attention to both pre-service and in-service training.

Unwillingness of the Professional Staff to Accept Help

The greatest deterrent to the use of auxiliary personnel in the schools is that of teacher hesitancy to accept help on the grounds that they are not properly trained. Incredible as it is to hold this view in light of the knowledge explosion, it is nevertheless the case. Supervisors have a great responsibility to help the professional staff see the contributions that can be made by auxiliary personnel.

Human Relationships

The use of auxiliaries in the school brings people into very close contact with each other. Oftentimes these people do not have the communications skills to cope with the problems that result from such close contact. Therefore, a constant effort to improve communications must accompany any program that brings the teachers out of their "sacred portal."

Models for Tutor Programs

Tutor programs can be organized in a variety of ways. Following are examples of those most frequently used:

Structured Tutoring

Structured tutoring is a model for tutoring that is designed to cope with the unique learning characteristics of low-achieving students who are considered high risk in terms of school failure. It is usually closely supervised by an adult with experience in devising diagnostic criterion reference pre-tests, preparing and maintaining record sheets and instructional materials, and selecting and training tutors. The tutor is asked to follow a rather strict program as laid out by the teacher. Upper elementary students are usually used as tutors, although parents and secondary students have also been used. Pre-service and in-service training are important components of structured tutoring. The training usually consists of training in structured tutoring techniques and teaching the prescriptions which constitute criteria objectives for each child.

A structured tutoring project by Harrison and Brimley, called "The Use of Structured Tutoring Techniques in Teaching Low Achieving Six Year Olds to Read," was devised to teach reading to thirty-five six-year-old children who were considered low achievers on the basis of kindergarten testing. They used upper elementary students as tutors and implemented the program for six weeks. The children were tested at the end of this period. The primary teachers in the three participating schools were asked to rank all of their pupils on reading ability three months after the beginning of the school year. This ranking disclosed that only five of the children in the study were considered to be in the lower one-third of their class, in contrast to all thirty-three having been identified as being in the lower one-third of their kindergarten class.[4] Similar projects report success with underachieving students when a tightly programmed approach is used.

Tutoring with Technology

This tutoring technique attempts to teach by replacing the human intervention with a nonhuman one such as filmstrips, tapes, video tapes, computers, television, radio, and sometimes newspapers. Although used as a component in many tutoring programs, a pure technological tutoring program is best suited to those who do not need the support of a human. When the human factor is added to this technique it becomes a very powerful program.

Experiments conducted with this type of tutoring have produced some rather dramatic results. Strang, in a project called "An Automated Audio Visual Approach to Remediate Reading Problems," conducted three experiments over a period of two years with a group of sixth graders. In experiment number one he tested the effectiveness of exposure to graded reading materials and audio visual tutoring in an automated reading program with specific behavioral objectives and a self-contained rewards system. Twenty-one students formed three groups of equal reading proficiency. The group that received specific audio visual tutoring showed substantial gains in reading accuracy over the group receiving trial and error training in reading. In experiment number two the audio visual tutoring was administered to nineteen students, and the gains were compared to those students not receiving any machine instruction. Improvement in tutored students paralleled that of experiment number one. In experiment

---

[4]Vern Brimley and Grant Harrison, "The Use of Structured Tutoring Techniques in Teaching Low Achieving Six Year Olds to Read" (Paper presented at the meeting of the American Educational Research Association, New York, N.Y., February, 1971) ERIC (Ed. 047898).

number three, students participating in experiment two intermittently received automated instruction on several everyday reading skills. The tutored students' improvement across the year was significantly greater than those students receiving no tutoring.[5]

Computer Assisted Instruction is one piece of technology that has the greatest potential for tutoring, for it attacks one of the greatest problems in education—how to get sufficient variety in educational materials to teach each individual without requiring a group of trained personnel to prepare all possible variations.[6] Computer Assisted Instruction permits individualization electronically; it can be used to train in problem solving; for drill and practice; it responds to questions for simulation and gaming; it can be used for tutorial instruction. It also interacts with a student in a dynamic way and is responsive to him.

Again, pure Computer Assisted Instruction without the intervention of humans can be destructive. This can be overcome simply by adding the human component. At the present time, the limiting factor in the use of CAI is cost and not the lack of programs or its inhumaneness.

Study Center Tutoring

Study Center Tutoring is an approach that tries to remediate or enrich the child's education by bringing him into a setting built around certain experiences. These centers can be found in churches, community buildings, storefronts, or in the school itself. They usually operate after school and on weekends, and are most often manned by paid professional staff or volunteer lay professionals. Depending upon the type of program to be offered, these centers are equipped with reference materials, audio visual materials, and individual study space. Sometimes a stations approach is used whereby a child, upon finishing one set of objectives, can move on to the next station. Usually the purpose of these study centers is to help children feel more self-confident in the basic skills and more positive about themselves. The center is not a drop-in for anyone who has no other place to go. Rather, it is an

[5]Harold Strang, *An Automated Audio Visual Approach to Remediate Reading Problems* (July, 1971) ERIC (Ed. 955764).

[6]Lawrence Stolurow, *Computer Assisted Instruction: Education Automation Monograph Series* (Grosse Pointe, Michigan: American Data Processing, Inc., 1968) ERIC (Ed. 028649).

after-school extension of the instructional program for the children who need it. Tutors work both on a one-to-one basis and with small groups in the centers.

Study Centers are particularly good for children of minorities who may not have proper places to study or no one to help them. For instance, migrant children whose parents work in the fields until late at night have had these centers set up for them. For added motivation, the children sometimes work for tokens that can later be redeemed at a store for personal items such as toothbrushes, soap, school supplies, and food. This is a particularly good way to provide both for physical as well as intellectual needs.

Most of these centers are staffed on a voluntary basis. Sometimes through the cooperation of philanthrophic organizations, VISTA, NYC, or various title programs, these centers can pay both the tutor and the teacher.

Home Based Tutoring

Home Based Tutoring is most often implemented to raise the literacy level of disadvantaged parents and children by offering tutoring services to both. Nonprofessionals either tutor the child in the home with the parent observing, and sometimes supplementing the instruction, or teach the parent directly and have no contact with the child. In some cases, the parent is trained to be the tutor. The programs most often include such things as child growth and development, child care, birth control, language training, conceptual training and sensory-motor training.

Important to the success of this program is being able to develop rapport with the home and having a sound program of pre-service and in-service training, especially if parents are to be used as tutors.

Studies have shown that the time variable for attitudinal change is quite long with disadvantaged parents. In a study by Badger, called "Mothers' Training of the Group Process," he found the following when training mothers to care better for their children:

> Twenty mothers, all Aid to Dependent Children recipients, agreed to meet for classes two hours per week to learn teaching techniques to apply at home. These meetings included instruction

in child-centered activities such as how to profitably use educational toys and materials, child management and birth control. The second year of the program they suggested the mothers begin using positive reinforcement in dealing with their children, show interest in their learning and give the children experience in problem solving. Study results showed that the children had made significant gains both in the Stanford-Binet and the ITPA. The mothers showed much interest in the program, attended regularly, and became involved as tutors with the children. Observations of home visits indicated that the mothers' attitudes changed positively in respect to the teacher of their infants. The study concluded that parents must be included in programs for the disadvantaged and that the time variable is crucial to attitude change since it was the beginning of the second year before the mothers developed enough self-confidence to use at home what they had learned in class.[7]

Then too there is the question of when it is appropriate to intervene with disadvantaged children. Some studies indicate they have worked with two- to four-year-olds and found it to be too late. A Home Tutoring study by Schaefer and Aaronson indicated that intervention before the child was fourteen months was necessary to provide for the deficiency of disadvantaged children.[8]

As indicated earlier, disadvantaged mothers can be used as tutors only if they are trained. In a study by Bushell and Jacobson, called "The Simultaneous Rehabilitation of Mothers and Their Children," it was found that disadvantaged mothers oftentimes made irrelevant and negative comments when tutoring. Written explanations at various study areas were to no avail. Only when they used tele-coaching over earphones did the mothers' behavior change.[9] This is well to remember when implementing any tutor program that attempts to upgrade the skills of the tutor.

---

[7] Earladeen Badger, *Mothers' Training Program of the Group Process* (July, 1969) (Ed. 932926).

[8] Mary Aaronson and Earl Schaefer, "Infant Education Research Project: Implementation and Implications of a Home Tutoring Program" (New York, N.Y., Ronald K. Parker Ed., City University of New York, 1970) ERIC (Ed. 054875).

[9] Don Bushell and Joan Jacobson, "The Simultaneous Rehabilitation of Mothers and Their Children" (Paper presented at the meeting of the Psychological Association, San Francisco, California, August 30, 1968) ERIC (Ed. 034591).

Homework Helper Program

Homework Helper tutoring can, and oftentimes does, combine several of the other models. Sometimes high school students will work with the tutee in his classroom during or after school, or work in the tutee's home on work the teacher has assigned. The Study Center model is also used in this program. Most of the time the tutor is under the direction of a master teacher and carries out her directions. As in most other forms of tutoring, the thrust is in the area of basic skills and self-image, together with the identification of a positive role model. The disadvantage of the Homework Helper Program is the tendency of contact between the tutor and the teacher to drop off after the initial matching.

On Demand Tutoring

Perhaps the most frequently used model, and the least beneficial in terms of sustained gain, is that of On Demand Tutoring. This model develops as the classroom program changes. If a few of the children in a classroom are having a problem with something, the teacher will schedule some older students to come in at certain times of the day to help. Or maybe the teacher has more centers of interest than she can handle. She will arrange for an older boy or girl to come in and work at the center for as long as she needs them. The advantage of this program is the extra help provided which gives children more learning options. The disadvantage is the program becomes fragmented and no lasting relationship develops between the tutor and tutee.

Whole Class One-to-One Tutoring

Whole class tutoring is an attempt to match whole classes of tutors with whole classes of tutees for the purpose of improving basic skills, improving self image, and developing within the tutor a caring attitude for young children.

An Operational Plan

Three staff members at Kelly School, seeing the disadvantages of the On Demand tutoring program, decided to see what would happen if they matched seventy-five kindergarten and Primary III children with seventy-five Intermediate Six children. The program developed as follows:

A. Each tutor was assigned a tutee from kindergarten or Primary III on the basis of mutual interests, skill needs, and friendships. In all cases one agreed they wanted to work with the other.

B. The program took place each day for four months from 11:00AM-11:40AM and 2:45PM-3:25PM. This was found to be advantageous both from the standpoint of clean-up and the flexibility it gave the afternoon program.

C. The tutor worked with the tutee four days of each week and the fifth day was used for teacher-tutor planning. The teacher of the tutees met with the tutors who worked with her children and gave them ideas about what to do with the tutees. The teacher of the tutors went to the tutees' room and worked with them. This worked well for two reasons: The teacher of the tutees found this to be a good planning session. The teacher of the tutors used this as an opportunity to interact with young children who had never been exposed to men teachers.

D. Besides this day of planning, the teachers would meet independently on various days and assess the program needs. They made up idea books for the tutors and lesson plans for the next week. They also used the time the tutor and tutee worked together for planning and helping them with various problems that came up.

Sample Lesson Plans for Kindergarten Tutees

Week I

Team Room Tutors

Your tutee's name _____

Do each of the items and check that item when it is completed:

___Teach tutee to write his last name, address, and phone number.

Find in Math Center

___Have the tutee complete (6) tangram patterns.

___Write his numbers as far as he can go. Try to write (1-20)

___Use the balance scale. Ask the tutee which weighs more, a crayon or a pencil; one large block or two small blocks, etc. Check to find out.

Find in Writing Center

___Play the visual discrimination game. (Played like Concentration.)
___Play Concentration with cards on beginning sounds.

Reading Center

___Read a story to the tutee.
___Print in manuscript on a sheet of paper what he tells you about that story.

Gym Outside

___Take your tutee outside each nice day for 10-15 minutes.
___Do attached worksheet.

Worksheet

Complete this pattern

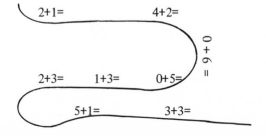

Tutor's Name_____

Figure 2-1

Week II

Team Room Tutors

Your tutee's name _____
Do each of the items and check that item when it is completed:

Mathematics

___Prepare the following game on a sheet of large construction paper. Write combinations *without* answers. The tutee supplies the answer as he races an object on the track. If he doesn't know the answer, his car breaks down and he starts all over again. Tell him the answer he doesn't know.

$$2+1= \qquad 4+2=$$

$$9+0=$$

$$2+3= \qquad 1+3= \qquad 0+5=$$

$$5+1= \qquad 3+3=$$

Language Arts

___Prepare a story to tell to your tutee. Your story will have some parts that are not related to the story. When you tell those parts that are unrelated, the child makes a sound using an instrument. Example: drum, triangle, etc. Next, he tells you a story with unrelated parts, and you make noise with an instrument.

___Ask the tutee if he can read. If he can, ask him to read from his book to you.

___You read a story to your tutee. Ask him questions about the story.

___Use the Borg-Worner System 80 with your tutee.

Art

___(Find in the art center) Use burlap, yarn, needle and dowel (stick). Make a tapestry for the tutee's mother. *Both* of you sew on the burlap at the same time. Keep finished project in school.

___Q-tips and tempera are needed for this project. Dip the Q-tips in tempera. Dab on to white construction paper to make your design.

Tutor's Name_____

Figure 2-2

Week III

Team Room Tutors

Your tutee's name _____
Do each of the items and check that item when it is completed.

Mathematics

___The tutor draws 10 pictures on construction paper. The tutor numbers them first, second, etc. The tutor cuts them apart and mixes them up. Have the tutee arrange them in order.

x:	First	Second	Third	Fourth	Fifth	Sixth	Seventh	Etc.

Do this activity until the tutee gets it correct and knows the words.

___Go to the math center (   ) and have the tutee tell time for you on any of the clocks available. Work with just the hour unless the tutee wants to learn the 1/2 hour. Ex: 10 o'clock, 12 o'clock, etc.

Language Arts

___Make the same race track that you made last week using words instead of numbers. Go over this track as often as it takes for your tutee to learn these words listed. *Use construction paper.*

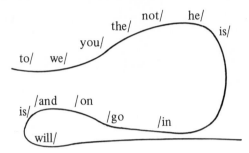

The tutee may take this car home *if* he knows all the words on the track. (Cut out the car.)

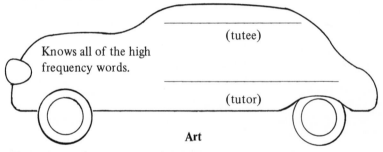

Art

___Place about 1/2 cup fingerpaint into a cookie sheet. Have the tutee move the paint around with his hands and make a design. Now lay a sheet of fingerpaint paper, *shiny side down,* on top of the design. Rub the paper lightly with your hand. Presto! the design will transfer onto the paper. Lift up the paper and hang it in the cloakroom to dry. Place paint back into the jar. Please clean up!

___Play a classroom game.

___Work with System 80.

___Put on a puppet show.

___Read to the tutee. Have him read to you.

___Go outside for a walk.

___Bring a picnic lunch for yourself and your tutee. Eat near the track area.

___Check other checklists for ideas.

Tutor's Name_____

Figure 2-3

Week IV

Team Room Tutors

Your tutee's name _____

Do each of the items and check that item when it has been completed.

Art

___Do tie dyeing. Remember to tie your material with rubber bands so that your project is dyed different colors for each tie that you've made with the rubber bands. (Soak your finished project in vinegar and water to set the color. Ring out, hang in the cloakroom.)

___Find twigs, bark, leaves, etc. Bring to school. Use glue and paste onto the bird picture that the tutee chooses. The bird pictures are in the ▭ center.

___Find a spider, ant, bee, etc. Place in any type of jar. Have the tutee write a language experience story about the insect. (Where the insect was found, what the insect eats, how he would feel if he were that insect, how he would protect himself from his enemies.)

___Make a book marker. Use the corner of an envelope that has been cut for you. Decorate the book marker with drawings.

Language Arts

___Make this game:

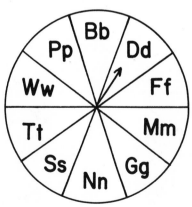

Put a pointer on the game. Make small cards of letters Dd, Ff, Mm, Gg, Nn, Ss, Tt, Ww, Pp, and Bb. Place cards face down. Turn over the card. Name it. Find the letter on the circle with the pointer. What starts with that letter? Practice until your child knows all letters on the game.

Mathematics

___Pegboard Patterns. Ask your tutee to get a pegboard and pegs from the ◇ center. Reproduce the patterns that I have prepared by placing pegs into the pegboard. Reproduce five patterns.

___Geoboards. Ask your tutee to find 2 geoboards and 8 rubber bands in the ◇ center. The tutor makes geometric figures using rubber bands and the tutee reproduces those figures. Ask the tutee what shapes he has made. (squares, rectangles, octagons, etc.)

Tutor's Name _____

Figure 2-4

I feel great when I teach something
to someone else.

You make the letter this way.

Figure 2-5

My tutee seems to learn far more
when I use concrete objects.

Moms fit right into the tutor program

A little technology doesn't hurt either.

There should be more opportunities for big kids to make friends with little kids.

Figure 2-6

Let's look through the folder and see what we should do.

These little kids can really make nice things.

E. Each tutor had a folder that he kept of all the work of the tutee. He would correct it, many times with the tutee, make comments, and sometimes write notes to the parents on ways he felt they could reinforce what was being done in the tutor program. The folder also contained a ditto list of instructional experiences that had been made up by the teachers. As the program developed, it was found that the tutor could also find appropriate instructional experiences to strengthen a skill deficiency.

F. The tutors and tutees worked in any area of the school that was not used for anything else. Some chose to work in the classroom because of the blackboards, audio visual equipment, and materials that were easily obtained. Others worked in the court, on the playground, on the stage, in the gym, the kitchen, or in the corridors, depending upon the areas they were trying to develop.

The main problem with a project as large as this was that of trying to determine the individual needs of such a large group, and find appropriate activities for them. The teachers used their own files, idea books that have been written on games, and ideas that were developed during the project. At the end of four months, the teachers put together the various ideas that developed and made an idea book of their own, called *Passing on Knowledge*. This will make any future tutoring projects significantly easier to provide for the needs of the participants.

Evaluating the Program

Although no formal evaluation took place, many interesting things were observed. Almost at once, the teachers could see the helping relationship develop between the tutor and the tutee. There seemed to be far fewer incidents of big kids teasing and picking on the little ones. The young children began to see the older children as helpers and someone to model. Children were often seen touching each other, holding hands while walking down the halls, and it wasn't uncommon for the tutee to be sitting in the lap of the tutor while being instructed. On stormy days the tutor showed his concern by walking children to their homes or helping them to an awaiting bus. On lyceum days the tutor and the tutee sat together. No longer did the staff have to control and admonish during a performance. The teachers remarked they had never witnessed such a caring on the part of older children for younger ones.

Although there was no formal pre-testing or post-testing of skills, the teachers felt there were significant gains in such areas as forming letters, knowledge of the alphabet, psychomotor development, following directions and attitudes about school and other people. They also felt the writing of the tutor improved as a result of spending a great deal of time taking dictation for language experience stories.

Parents seemed better informed about school than ever before. Both the tutor and the tutee talked a great deal about this program at home, as evidenced by the comments of parents. "Who is this tutor my boy is talking about?" "My child has really opened up since the start of the tutor program." "My child knows his alphabet, can read better, or likes school better" were some of the comments heard with great frequency.

Chapter 3

Training the Tutor

It should not be assumed that tutors can suddenly appear in the school and, without training, make impact upon the educational program.

It is true that everyone who enters a school is a unique resource of his own feelings and perceptions. He may even have some unique skills that he performs better than anyone else. For instance, the tutor who has just won a trip to the National Science Fair with his project on aerodynamics will probably do a better job of helping the children with building model airplanes than any of the teachers. However, because of the uniqueness and complex-ity of many school tasks, the tutor will need some specialized training. Therefore, it is recommended that pre-service and in-service training be a component in any tutor program.

The purpose of this chapter is to expose the tutor, or any other auxiliary, to some of the more important concepts of dealing with young children.

The chapter begins with a short description of *Action Impera-tives for Modern Schools*. This is an attempt to give the tutor some baseline information about the function of modern schools. For many of the tutors it will have been their first exposure to an elementary school since they were a student in one.

Tutors need to know how to build a cohesive feeling with children. Reflective listening is included because it has been found to be a good technique to both build cohesion and relate to children in more positive ways.

Tutors should have some knowledge of human growth and development because it will help them determine the tutees' readiness for various activities.

Dr. James Smith's lists of *Principles of Creative Teaching* have been included because they seem to be a convenient springboard to a discussion of what creativity is all about.

Few techniques have the potential of being as valuable to the tutor as role playing. Learning this process will help the tutor more easily find role and make the whole process of tutoring much more fun.

Numerous other things have been included, such as audio visual training, tutor checklists, and evaluation, because they seem to be things that need to be considered in any tutor program.

Tutor training will be different in each school. The resources available, the nature of the tutors, and the desires of the school staff will make each tutor training program unique. It is hoped that some of the concepts presented here will be included when implementing a tutor program.

Action Imperatives for Modern Schools

There are certain imperatives that are part of every good school. Because tutors are often far removed from schools, it is recommended that someone give a presentation that will help them get an idea of what is currently taking place in schools. The discussion might center around the acronym ACTION.

Auxiliary Program

The auxiliary program is that effort to remove from the professional staff all things not directly related to diagnosis and prescription. It is a concerted effort to harness all available resources in such a way as to maximize interaction between the child and his teacher(s).

Cooperative Supervision

Time and time again, studies reaffirm the high positive correlation between a good school and the presence of a good leader.[1] The supervisory program is that plan which provides for the improvement of instruction.

Teaching and Learning

This is the substance of what the school is about. It is that effort to structure a tailor-made program for each child. This imperative is accomplished only to the degree that adequate attention is given to each of the others.

Involvement of the Community

Change in the school program makes community involvement an imperative. Then too, the community represents one of the largest untapped resources available to teachers.

Organization of the School

A modern school is organized around student needs. Increasingly, educators are seeing team teaching, differentiated staffing, and multi-age grouping as the organization that best meets the needs of children.

Nurturing Humaneness

All of the other imperatives bring people into much closer relationships with each other than ever before. Therefore, it is important that human development programs be implemented in an effort to help people relate in better ways.

The Importance of Tutor Training

The success or failure of tutor programs rests almost entirely upon the ability of the professional staff to implement a sound program of pre-service and in-service training. Without this

---

[1]Donald Mitchell, *Leadership in Public Education Study* (Washington, D.C.: Academy for Educational Development, Inc., 1972), p. 13.

training, the program can be little more than attacking surface problems.

Insofar as training is concerned, much of it is the same as that participated in by the professional staff. Therefore, it is important that each tutor be committed to participation in as much teacher in-service as possible.

Each tutor should have a notebook or file in which to organize all he learns. For instance, it is not uncommon for supervisors to funnel a constant stream of creative ideas to their teachers. The tutor, too, should get these ideas and have them organized in such a way that they can be used when the need arises.

Building Cohesion

One of the most important components of tutor training is that of building cohesion with the tutor and helping him build cohesion with his tutee. Cohesion is simply providing the opportunity for groups or individuals to get so involved with each other that they begin to see each other as persons, and therefore invest interest in each other.[2]

How is this accomplished? First, it is important to use activities that are so powerful that they cause people to get off the cognitive level of relationships and onto the feeling level. Questions like, "What did you do this summer?" "How long was your vacation?" and "Where are you going next summer?" are not the kinds of questions that will stimulate or kick off feelings.

Self Enhancing Education educators have structured many activities based upon feelings that will help build investment of interest. Some are presented below as ideas to help groups or individuals build and maintain a cohesive feeling.

Who am I?

What are you feeling and perceiving?
What do you have concerns about?
What do you feel good about?
How are we alike?

---

[2]Norma Randolph, William Howe and Elizabeth Achterman, *Self Enhancing Education: A Training Manual* (Santa Clara, California: Self Enhancing Education, Inc., 1971), p. 119.

How are we different?

Write everything you can about "me."

Where are we in time and space?

How important is it to know where we are?

Where are we this morning in time and space?

What do we know that wasn't known a few years ago?

What are some of the ways we can keep track of ourselves?

How does the calendar help us? The clock?

Why are we here?

Why do you come to school?

What does expectation mean?

Who has expectations for us?

What does the culture expect of us?

What does our government expect of us?

What are our goals for the year?

What are our operational problems?

How do we want the room arranged?

Where do we want to work?

How can we schedule our work?

How can we manage ourselves?

How can we solve problems that might come up with other students?

What activities will lead us toward our goal?

How can we help ourselves grow and assess our growth?

What is the relationship between growth and goals?

What does it mean to fulfill needs?

Do we have unmet needs? What are they?

Can we build a positive self-image?

Can we create change?

Can we improve communication?

Can we evaluate our self-management?

Can we overcome misbehavior?[3]

Reflective Listening

Reflective listening is a Self Enhancing Education technique that can be used to help people build cohesion. Following is their explanation of what it involves:

---

[3]*Self Enhancing Education,* Norma Randolph and William Howe, 1966 Educational Progress Corporation, p. 119-126.

In our traditional culture, we have not learned to listen effectively to one who is sending a message. We have not learned to listen to the perception and feelings of another person, and have not responded to him in such a way that he knows we have heard him. We traditionally judge his perception of feeling, right or wrong, good or bad, and then agree or disagree. What we have really done is to leave out a very important step in the communication process. This omission has frequently blunted two-way communication. We can find many illustrations around us of this blunting communication—divorce, generation gap, alienation of youth, rebellion and unhappy individuals.

We believe that the skill which we call reflective listening is a way to take care of the missing step. Reflective listening is becoming aware of feelings and perceptions that we read in another person's verbal or nonverbal messages and presenting them without judgment for corroboration. It requires the listener to really listen and put into his own words the feeling or perception of the sender's message. By so doing he lets the sender know that he has been heard and gives him an opportunity to confirm or deny the accuracy of the receiver's listening.

To adequately hear the message intended by the sender, the receiver has to hold in abeyance or suspend his own feelings and perceptions. Then he can feed back the message to check his accuracy and assure the listener that he has heard him.[4]

To demonstrate this technique of reflective listening, ask the members of a group or an individual to build a collage. A collage is an activity that asks participants to paste together an assortment of materials that make an artistic composition. Although it is particularly good to show the building of cohesiveness, it is also fun and deeply involves the participants.

When the collage is completed, you might ask, "What are you feeling and perceiving?" The conversation could go something like this:

Tutor: I went through the catalogs and magazines to find people in as many action positions as possible. I cut out the pictures and pasted them on the paper in all sorts of funny ways. I did this to show that I am concerned about the human race. I don't think people know where they are going or how they are going to get there. I pasted them close together because of the way people live in our country.

---

[4]Norma Randolph, William Howe and Elizabeth Achterman, "Self Enhancing Education: Reflective Listening" (Santa Clara, California: S.E.E., Inc., 1969), p. 6.

Teacher: Sounds like you are pretty upset about where we are heading?

Tutor: Yes, the pace is too fast. I think we need more time to relax and find time for ourselves.

Teacher: I thought I also heard a concern about overpopulation. I bet you would favor Zero Population Growth?

Tutor: No, not at all. My concern is not for the population as a whole. I am concerned about having so many people living in such small areas.

Teacher: Like Los Angeles or New York?

Tutor: Yes.

Teacher: The pollution is pretty bad in some of our larger cities.

Tutor: It sure is. Yesterday I heard a scientist talk about the smog in Los Angeles. I really got concerned when he said that technology will not get us out of this mess. He said it will take massive concern on the part of all of us. Los Angeles has over 100 days of smog at the present time. If we apply all of the technology we know, we will still have half that many days of smog by the turn of the century. I can't understand why some feel that technology can get us out of this mess.

Teacher: You can't legislate pollution away?

Tutor: No, I feel it is kind of an affair of the heart. Each of us must do our part.

Teacher: That was a good exchange, Mary. Do you feel heard?

Tutor: Yes, I sure do.

In reflective listening, the receiver of the message, in an effort to filter out all of the perceptions of the sender, must try to become aware of the other person's verbal and nonverbal messages and try to present them without judgment. As soon as you judge, the process is blunted.

In the second exchange, the receiver discovered that his perception was faulty. He felt the sender was concerned about overpopulation and found that he was concerned about large aggregations of people in small areas and the resulting pollution. By clearing up that false perception immediately, it allowed them to communicate in a way that perception was accurate for both the sender and the receiver.

How can this be used to build cohesion? First, when two people or a group of people are communicating in such a way that few power struggles develop, a feeling of trust begins to build. As other members of the group see this they begin to feel comfortable and they too want to enter into the conversation. When members of the group stop making all of the exchanges between the leader and themselves and begin to reflect each other, the process begins to solidify—a cohesive feeling begins to develop.

This does not complete the process of communication. To stop at this point is to only hear the feeling, and does not necessarily solve the problem. When all of the perception of the sender has been filtered out through the art of reflective listening, the receiver states his feeling condition. Upon stating his feeling condition, he seeks corroboration by asking for a way to solve the problem. Self Enhancing Education educators call this the "Angle of Dilemma."[5]

Age Characteristics of Students

For many tutors, this will be the first formal teaching experience they have ever had. So it is necessary to review the age characteristics of children and youth.

As you read these characteristics of each age level, you will no doubt see characteristics that do not match a given child in your class. The lists of characteristics should not be taken that literally. They are simply generalizations based upon large groups of children.

Below is a list of characteristics for each age level that has been compiled from the experiences of researchers and teachers over a period of many years. Read them carefully and try to make generalizations based upon the characteristics of each age group:

Five Year Old

> Nice—wants to be told what to do and does it gladly
> Period of slow growth—girls usually ahead of boys in physical development
> Good motor control—sure of his movements—needs a lot of big muscle activity
> Sensory equipment not ready for close work

---

[5] Randolph, Howe and Achterman, *Self Enhancing Education: A Training Manual*, p. 64

Eye-hand coordination improving but still not good
Good health
Very home centered—likes to stay close to Mom
Can be overwhelmed by too much noise or too much bigness
Is ready for group activities
Handedness established
Wants to learn—especially wants to learn to read
At five and one-half he is not so cooperative anymore—he has more power struggles with his parents and seeks more independence

Six Year Old

He replaces mother as the center of all things
Exuberant—restless—overactive and loud
Oftentimes thought to be selfish by those around him
Cannot participate in team sports because of his desire to win
Desires praise and needs it more than at any level
Not so sure of his movements now
Can be a behavior problem if outlet is not found for his overactivity
Very eager to learn
Uses energy at such a rate that he fatigues easily—the typical school day is too long
Not so resistent to illness
Short attention span

Seven Year Old

Much more withdrawn than at six—will take his displeasure out on himself rather than that which displeases him
Sensitive to criticism
Loves to write and draw—strives for perfection
Needs approval from adults
Can get very absorbed in books
Has many fears about small things
Tries so hard he oftentimes gets ill
Loves to work at the chalkboard
Is getting much better at controlling himself
Has a strong attachment to peers and his teachers
Learns best when things are concrete
Better eye-hand coordination but still not ready for close work
May steal to win love or approval

Eight Year Old

Is developing more stamina
Can focus on close work better
Improved health
Manipulative skills are better
Can express himself better
Likes to work in groups and has a strong desire to organize clubs
Eye-hand coordination developing to the point of being able to do close work
Can attack words well
Longer attention span
Can be very critical of those who keep him waiting
Gang develops—best friend of the same sex
Academic problems will surface as behavioral problems
Careless with personal items
Beginning to show an interest in dramatics
Interest in team sports

Nine Year Old

Girls speed ahead of boys in physical maturity
Becoming very independent and needs much less supervision and control
Can easily focus on close work
Seeks friends of the same sex and enjoys hobbies, Scouts, etc.
Sometimes overdoes involvement in outside activities
Very concerned about peer relationships
Loves to compete in team sports—often argues about the rules
Loves to read with prolonged interest—enjoys self selection in reading
Becoming aware of differences in boys and girls physically and academically
Is developing thinking skills—much more independent in his work
Not as critical of his peers as before

Ten Year Old

Much more relaxed than before, good natured, nice to have around
Close to his mom, like the fives
Doesn't like highly structured or planned activities
Has many interests
Loves to watch TV and can remember minute details
Perfecting play skills

Likes oral work better than written—loves to talk to anyone about anything
Loves to read—hero worship—great men
Likes to write but has trouble organizing his thoughts
Easily distracted
Not so critical of himself
Gang is strong

Preadolescence (9-13)

Boys mature as much as two years later than girls
Secondary sex characteristics begin to appear
Wide range of maturity level
Interest in team sports is intense—girls love to mix it up
Marked difference in the interests of boys and girls
Love to tease
Awkward—restless and sometimes lazy because of rapid growth
Seeks peer approval more than parents or teachers
Changeable—sometimes uncooperative and rebellious
Interest in career beginning to develop—earning money
Want adults to relate to them in adult ways

Adolescence

Rapid weight gain—enormous appetite
Sexual maturity with accompanying physical and emotional changes
Muscular coordination improved
Goes to extremes—sometimes has a know-it-all attitude
Daydreams
Great interest in the affairs of the world
Very identity-oriented—Who am I? Where am I going? What can I do?
Wants to be popular
Strongly independent
Hero worhsip of admired adult
Loves to work in groups which can form cliques
Great interest in physical activities
Girls more interested in boys than boys in girls
Must be related to in adult ways

Material Adapted From:

A. Interviews with Staff Members
B. Ilg, Francis and Louise Bates Ames, *School Readiness,* New York, N.Y.: Harper and Row Publishers, Inc., 1965.
C. Jenkins, Gladys, Helen Schacter and William Bauer, *These are Your Children,* Dallas, Texas, Scott Foresman, Inc., 1966.

For information on the age characteristics of children younger than five see:

A. Fraiberg, Selma, *The Magic Years,* New York, N.Y.: Charles Scribner's Sons, 1959.

As you read the age characteristics you probably found items that could be added for some of the age groups, or maybe you felt some were out of place. Based upon your experience, make a list of your own.

Another way of using this list is to give it to a group of tutors and ask them to give you several ideas for working with their tutees based upon the age characteristics.

Creativity

A tremendous amount of research has been accumulated over the past several years in the area of creativity and creative teaching. Dr. James Smith, in his book *Creative Teaching of Reading and Literature in the Elementary School,* has done a superior job of summarizing the basic principles of creativity and how they apply to creative teaching. They are listed below with the hope of helping tutors to apply these principles when they work with their tutees:

Basic Principles of Creativity

1. All children are born creative.
2. There is a relationship between creativity and intelligence; highly creative people are always intelligent, though highly intelligent people are not always creative. But all children can create to some degree.
3. Creativity is a form of giftedness which is not measured by current intelligence tests.
4. All areas of the curriculum may be used to develop creativity.
5. Creativity is a process and a product.
6. Creativity is developed by focusing on those processes of the intellect which fall under the general area of divergent thinking. This area of the intellect has been greatly neglected in our teaching up to this point.
7. All creative processes cannot always be developed at one time or in one lesson. Lessons must be planned to focus on each process.
8. Creativity cannot be taught; we can only set conditions for it

to happen in and insure its reappearance through reinforcement.

9. More knowledge, more skills, and more facts than ever before are required for creativity to be developed.

10. The theories of creative development lead us to believe that children must be able to tap all of life's experiences in order to become truly creative; unnecessary rules and actions may force much of their experience into the preconscious, where it cannot be readily used.

11. Excessive conformity and rigidity are true enemies of creativity.

12. Children go through definite steps in the creative process.

13. Creative teaching and creative learning can be more effective than other types of teaching and learning.

14. Children who have lost much of their creativity may be helped to regain it by special methods of teaching.

Basic Principles of Creative Teaching

1. Something new, different, or unique results.

2. Divergent thinking processes are stressed.

3. Motivational tensions are a prerequisite to the creative process; the process serves as a tension-relieving agent.

4. Open-ended situations are utilized.

5. There comes a time when the teacher withdraws and children face the unknown themselves.

6. The outcomes are unpredictable.

7. Conditions are set which make possible preconscious thinking.

8. Students are encouraged to generate and develop their own ideas.

9. Differences, uniqueness, individuality and originality are stressed and rewarded.

10. The process is as important as the product.

11. Certain conditions must be set to permit creativity to appear.

12. It is success rather than failure oriented.

13. Provision is made for learning knowledges and skills, but provision is also made to apply these to new, problem-solving situations.

14. Self-initiated learning is encouraged.

15. Skills of constructive criticism and evaluation are developed.

16. Ideas and objects are manipulated and explored.

17. It employs democratic processes.[6]

For the purposes of discussion, select a statement like "All children are born creative" and ask the tutors how this applies to their work with tutees. A study of several of them could give tutors a lot of insight into the creative process.

Role Playing

For most, the role of tutor is a new one. Something needs to happen to make the tutor feel comfortable in his new role. Role playing, or acting out situations or problems in a friendly setting, can do just that. Following are some of the reasons why this can be a very effective training device:

A. Role playing is a good way to develop instant cohesion between groups or individuals.
B. Learning is rapid, and doesn't fall off because of the deep involvement of the players.
C. Role playing can help the tutor develop feeling for others.
D. Role playing capitalizes on play, one of the child's most useful techniques in learning.
E. Tutors learn to anticipate problems through role playing.
F. Role playing can build confidence in the players.
G. Role playing can build awareness in the players.
H. Role playing is a good technique to help us laugh at ourselves.

Hints to Help Role Playing

When working with a group of tutors who have had no experience with role playing, it is necessary to spend some time discussing its purposes. After a short discussion, sample the tutors' feelings by asking, "What are you feeling and perceiving?" or "What do you feel good about and what do you have concerns about?" Using the technique of reflective listening will enable you to stimulate a lot of conversation about role playing and help to develop a cohesive feeling among the group.

---

[6]*Creative Teaching of Reading and Literature in the Elementary School* (Boston, Mass.: Allyn and Bacon, Inc., 1966), p. 11-13, (Used by permission)

After all members feel pretty good about what they are about to attempt, it will be advisable to role play some situations not directly related to the tutor-tutee relationship. Using the technique of reflective listening, ask group members to role play the following real life situations or have them make up some of their own.

1. One brother is constantly wearing the other's clothing.
2. John is always left out of games.
3. Your brother gets the room messy and you get blamed for it.
4. Your teacher is concerned because you don't come to school on time.
5. You are telling your teacher that you got a poor score on your paper because you couldn't see the board.
6. You are in constant trouble in the playground.
7. Spelling is hard for you.
8. You have just told your teacher that you like the one you had last year much more.
9. An angry parent comes to the school because her child got pushed in the mud.

After the group feels comfortable with these roles, select some that are more directly related to the tutor-tutee relationship. Select one of your own or one from the following list:

1. Your tutee won't respond. What do you do?
2. You hear that your tutee is a behavior problem in the playground.
3. You are in a planning session with your tutee and he says, "I am never coming back to this class again!"
4. You have just met your new tutee.
5. Your tutee comes late to class.
6. Your tutee won't clean up after class.
7. You are the teacher and the tutor is not taking his responsibility very seriously.

When role playing, try to make the members feel as comfortable as possible. To begin with, it might be advisable for a group leader to role play with another group leader. Sometimes someone from the group may have had some role playing experience and want to volunteer. Never force people into role playing situations until they feel comfortable. Sometimes it is wise to break the group up into pairs and have them practice in private. Many will then want to present before the group.

Sometimes role playing is easier if there are props available. Dividers, old clothing like coats, hats, and shoes can be very helpful to both find and stay in role.

Situations to Avoid in Role Playing

Remember that all members of the group have certain responsibilities during role playing sessions. If two people are making an honest effort to play roles, the audience has the responsibility to support their effort.

When role playing it is important that neither of the players try to win. Oftentimes, because of insecurity and fear, one of the players may try to make the situation so difficult that the other member has a difficult time responding—and in the process, he comes out the winner. This should be avoided.

Breaking out of role is one of the most common problems when role playing. Again, this is done because one of the players has met a situation that he cannot handle, and he is trying to withdraw in an honorable way. This can be avoided if people are made to feel comfortable in the role playing sessions.

Evaluating Role Playing

Role playing is most beneficial when the sessions are evaluated. Devices like tape recorders, video tape equipment, and written comments are useful when evaluating role playing.

Again, reflective listening will be an effective device to insure an evaluation that leads both to improved role playing sessions and greater awareness on the part of the players.

Audio Visual Training

Most schools of today are filled with a wide assortment of audio visual equipment and materials. Because they are such an important part of the classroom program, tutors will need to know how to operate them. Therefore, workshops should be held periodically for the purpose of orienting tutors and tutees to audio visual equipment.

Fortunately many classroom teachers now allow students to use much of the equipment. Therefore, many of the tutors and tutees will know how to operate them. However, all tutors are not residents of a school. Disadvantaged mothers, lay persons, and college students who come in to the school to tutor will need extensive work in the operation of the equipment.

Tutors and Parents

For many parents, tutoring will be something new, and new things frighten people. Include parents in as much of the planning as possible. As soon as the program is underway, begin sending them information about the program and invite them in to participate in a tutoring session. It may be a good way to begin another tutoring program in your school.

Evaluating the Program

Process Steps in Role Playing

1. Social Structure of the Group
   A. Understanding of the basic values of the group
   B. Open or closed to new data
   C. How much will they reveal?
2. Problem
   A. Stated by the leader
   B. Felt need of group or group member
3. Choose Players
   A. Choose situation least threatening to group members. (Group leader role plays with a volunteer or two members role play in private and share before the group.)
4. Stable Limits
   A. Observers
      1) Non verbal clues support each player
   B. Players
      1) Won't break out of role
      2) Won't engulf each other
      3) All transactions will be as close to reality as possible.
5. Evaluation
   A. Observers interact with role players in a positive way.
   B. Transactions are saved and used later for discussion (tapes, video tapes, hand written notes).
6. Product
   A. Each player and member of the group is enlarged by the

process and has more understanding of problem solving through role playing.

Figure 3-1

Whenever embarking upon new programs it is well to think about evaluation. Too many programs are implemented and evaluated after the fact. Try to determine the program goals and set up an evaluation model to see if those goals have been met. Following is an example of the various pre-test - post-test information that could be valuable:

A. Draw Yourself
B. Samples of Work (letter formation, writing)
C. Attitude Scales
D. Standardized Tests
E. Teacher Comments
F. Tutor Comments
G. Tutee Comments
H. Parent Comments

During the time the tutor program is in operation, it is well to have an ongoing evaluation of the tutoring sessions. Following are examples of two forms that can be used to facilitate planning and evaluating readiness for tutoring.

Tutor Evaluation Sheet

Name of Tutor_____Age_____

Name of Tutee_____Age_____

Date_____ School_____

Skills to Teach:

Purpose:

Implementation Plan:

Materials Needed:

Evaluation:

Comments:

Improvements to be Made:

_____
(Signed)

Figure 3-2

Tutor Checklist *Personal*	Yes	No	Sometime:
Can I listen reflectively withholding judgment until I have heard all of the message?			
Do I keep in confidence that which the teacher or tutor does not want repeated?			
Do I have good self control when I am upset by something the tutee has done?			
Am I congruent with my feelings? (Does my verbal and nonverbal match)			
Am I confident in what I am doing?			
Am I neat in appearance when I work with my tutee?			
Am I enthusiastic?			
Am I dependable?			
Teaching Procedures Do I plan well?			
Do I motivate the tutee?			
Do I understand the place of manipulation and involvement in learning?			

Tutor Checklist			
Personal	Yes	No	Sometimes
Have I taken time to build cohesion with my tutee?			
Do I have knowledge of what I am teaching?			
Do I plan the tutee's program with the teacher?			
Am I building self image in the tutee?			

Figure 3-3

Tutee Inventory

Name_____ Age _____
School_____Grade _____ Date _____

1. What do you usually do: after school? in the evening? on weekends?
2. What time do you go to bed? When do you get up?
3. Do you have any brothers and sisters? Tell me about them.
4. Who is your best friend?
5. Do you have a nickname? What is it? Do you like it?
6. Do you belong to any clubs? Which ones?
7. Do you take special lessons?
8. What are your favorite hobbies?
9. Do you like movies? How often do you go?
10. Do you watch TV? How much per week?
11. What are your favorite programs?
12. Have you ever been to: a farm, the circus, a picnic, summer camp, or on a long trip?
13. Do you play baseball? Do you swim? Do you like to fish? What is your favorite sport?
14. Do you have pets? Which kinds? Tell me about them.
15. Do you have collections of things? Tell me about them.
16. What do you want to be when you grow up?
17. Is that what your parents want you to be?

18. Do you like school? Tell me about things like friends, homework and your school subjects.
19. Do your parents help you with school work?
20. Do you like to read? What has influenced you either liking or not liking reading?
21. Do you like to be read to?
22. What are your favorite books?
23. How many books would you guess you read in a week, month, year?
24. Do your parents read much?
25. Do you have a library card?
26. How often do you go to the library?
27. How many books do you own?
28. Do you read the newspaper?
29. Which magazines do you get at home?
30. What is your favorite children's magazine? (Highlights, Ranger Rick, Jack and Jill, Wee Wisdom, etc.)
31. Do you get any children's magazines at home?
32. Do you have an allowance? What do you do with it?
33. Do you ever earn any money? How do you spend it?
34. What would be your wish if you could have anything you want this very minute?
35. Draw a picture of yourself at home.

36. Draw a picture of yourself at school.

Figure 3-4

Tutee Attitude Inventory

Directions: This is a chance to tell me exactly how you feel. You may say anything you like, but it must be just what you think.

1. Today I feel_____
2. When it is time for me to see my tutor I_____
3. My parents think tutors_____
4. I get angry when_____
5. I wish my tutor knew_____
6. To be grown up_____
7. School is_____

It may be well to start small. If your school has had little or no involvement with parents, the response will be small. If ten parents agree to come to the school one or two mornings per week, you have the beginnings of a worthwhile program.

The old adage of starting where people are certainly applies here. If a parent is a former teacher she might begin working in the classrooms immediately. If, on the other hand, she has had no experience in the school, you might want to begin by having her do clerical work in the office. When she feels comfortable with this kind of contribution, she may want to involve herself with children. Libraries or resource centers may be the most appropriate involvement at this time. If successful in this role, she may want to work even more closely with children. In that case, schedule her in classrooms at regular intervals.

Figure 5-2
Mothers sure are friendly in the library.

Some of the volunteers may want a variety of involvement while others may want to devote full time to something like running the central library. In that case, arrange it. Make up a schedule for one month at a time and send it out so everyone will know what their schedule looks like for the next few weeks. Assure them that they can call in for a replacement whenever the need arises.

So the volunteer group will take quite a few different variations. Some will want to work only in the office. Some may want to run a certain portion of the school program, such as noon supervision or craft and hobby programs. Hopefully many will want to work closely with children, both in and out of the classroom.

Sample Volunteer Letter

September 1

Dear Parents:

The VISTC (Volunteers in Service to Children) program is beginning its sixth year. In the past this program has been a great success and an important factor in providing better education for your children.

For those who are new, VISTC is a volunteer agency of the J. Nelson Kelly PTA. It is made up of a group of mothers who have some spare time and wish to volunteer it to the education of their children. The tasks they perform are varied. Sometimes they prefer to work in the office and help with clerical work. At other times they prefer to work in classrooms or the school library.

We recognize that you are the best teachers your child will ever have. Therefore, we encourage you to become involved in the school program. For the past several years the VISTC people have completely run the school library. We estimate that last year they volunteered over 1,000 hours to the library. We also estimate that about 100 parents worked regularly in the classrooms.

If you are interested in the VISTC program, please fill out the bottom portion of this letter and return it to the school as soon as possible. If you have any questions, please feel free to call at any time.

Sincerely,

Jerry L. Abbott, Principal

. . . .

(Please tear off and return)

_____I would like to volunteer for the VISTC program.

Signed_____

(parent)

Figure 5-3

Evaluation of VISTC

Periodically, it is well to ask volunteers to evaluate their experiences in your school. Following are excerpts taken from parent evaluations:

> My duties during the year have been many and varied; some of them routine, some creative.
>
> I receive no monetary payment for the work I do. However, I am rewarded in numerous other ways. It gives a mother a great deal of satisfaction to see just how her children are being educated. It is rewarding when teachers and administrators thank you for helping them with some of their duties and responsibilities.
>
> I would recommend this experience for every mother. This gives one an opportunity to see first-hand the fine job which is being done in the school.
>
> The program is very worthwhile in that it relieves the teachers of much of the paperwork and busywork that takes so much time away from teaching and preparation.
>
> The work required of the volunteer should be interesting and varied, but require no specialization or particular training.
>
> The rising costs, the experiments in modern education, and many new ideas receive much discussion in our community. Perhaps a continued implementation of the volunteer program will improve public awareness of the problems faced in our schools.
>
> Because schools are the most important entity within our community, their problems should be our problems, and the volunteer program is a small step in this direction.

American Education Week

Each year, usually the fourth week in October, American Education Week is observed. The aim of this observance is to take one week per year and make a concentrated effort to let the public know what the schools are doing.

Since its beginning in 1921, American Education Week has become one of the biggest public relations activities of the schools. From the standpoint of national participation, the National

Education Association estimates that thirty-two million persons visit school and one hundred million are reached via the media.[2]

Schools simply cannot pass up this tremendous possibility for public relations. Plans must be made to make the most of this special week.

The usual reaction to this week is to have an open house and ask parents to visit classrooms. Rarely is there an attempt to deeply involve parents in the activities of the school during this week.

It is recommended that the leader of the school prepare a position statement with respect to various activities that teachers could become involved in with their students. Following is a sample statement that could be used:

October 11

To: All Staff Members
Re: American Education Week
From: Jerry

It hardly seems possible that American Education Week is nearly here. This year the week of October 24 to October 30 has been set aside by the National Education Association as the week for this special observance.

This year, as before, I will prepare a letter with a letterhead depicting the theme of AEW to send home with each child. We will also try to generate a daily theme that can be sent home with each child each day. As in years past, I would like to ask you to include as part of your classroom activities something that will make parents feel good about coming to the school on this occasion. I will list some of the things you might consider:

1. Send home a *did you know* letter to your parents. Did you know our classroom now has . . . a new project, some new students, a field trip planned, etc.

2. Have parents fill out a card on their visit. What did you like about the school? What improvements could the school make?

3. Invite grandparents, brothers and sisters, or any other non-parents to school.

---

[2]*National Education Association Observance Manual: A Guide to Organizing and Planning for American Education Week* (Washington, D.C.: National Education Association, 1971), p. 3.

4. Move your entire class to the mall of a shopping center and teach one day.

5. Make a display for a store depicting something of current educational interest.

6. Do something special for fathers. Have the children draw pictures of their fathers.

7. Make tape recordings for the parents or other visitors.

8. Make cards, posters and banners to commemorate the occasion.

9. Send invitations to city officials, school board members and interested service clubs to visit on these days.

10. Write provocative questions about education and put them on cards. Hang them around the school.

11. Using centers of interest, set up self-teaching stations around the school. Demonstrate modern techniques.

12. Invite parents to view a special lesson on something of interest.

13. Ask some parents to come in and be part of the team during American Education Week so other parents can see the potential of parents as teachers.

14. Have programs that entertain.

15. Have the children make up skits that depict something about the theme of the week.

16. Have the children write letters to the editor, cartoons, and news stories for possible publication in the local newspaper.

17. Make sure all parents and children have name tags for better interaction.

18. Have a mailbox in your room for comments from parents.

19. Use this week as a technique to recruit parents to work in your classroom. Have a display on the use of parents in the school and allow interested parents to sign up.

20. Plan a parents' exhibit. It could show various aspects of parents' jobs, hobbies and interests. It could be in the area of cooking, crafts, or art. Each item could bear the name of the parent and the child.

21. Invite parents to participate in a discussion of how school has changed from the days when they attended school.

22. Ask newspaper and television people to come into your classroom and report on the special activities of the week.

23. Videotape a complete lesson and have it playing in the cafeteria so parents can view it when they wish.

24. Videotape parents visiting the school during the week for

playback at a future PTA meeting. Let this springboard into a discussion about *Parents and the School.*

There are probably many more ideas that could be used to better observe this week. Please feel free to do whatever you can to better involve parents in your program. I hope we can share the successes and failures of this week.

Signed,

Jerry

Figure 5-4

Parents as Classroom Aides

The use of parents in the classroom should be the goal of any program of community involvement. Watching parents and teachers working side by side to help children is indeed refreshing. In this act lies the essence of what it means to form a true partnership between the home and the school. Some argue that parents are not equipped to teach in the classroom. Perhaps some may need training and guidance. Others are naturals in the classroom and can do many things better than the professionals. In a sound program of community involvement all people are viewed as potential resources.

Following is a list of things that parents have done successfully during the past several years:

drive and supervise individualized field trips
make instructional games
play instructional games with children
work with small groups
help individual children with handwriting
supervise and assist creative dramatics
operate AV equipment
make and use puppets
record language experience stories
show slides
serve as resource person for an entertainment activity
build bulletin boards
make flashcards and use them with small groups
talk to children
have children read to them
conduct science experiments

work at centers of interest
replenish centers of interest
give diagnostic tests
work with children on names, addresses, tying shoes, etc.
share unique backgrounds with parents
supervise cooking in the classroom

This list could go on and on. It is not a list of activities engaged in by parents only. The same activities could be performed by youth tutoring youth, student teachers from a university, teacher aides or the classroom teacher. Because of the various experiences and talents that all of these people bring to the classroom, it is difficult to say that one activity is the prerogative of one kind of person and one of the other.

Room Mothers

Few things have been more damaging to the program of community involvement than the typical utilization of room mothers. Generally two or three mothers are selected at the beginning of each year for each classroom. If used at all, they come to the classroom two or three times each year for classroom parties.

No attempt will be made here to list the various activities that could be performed by room mothers. In general, they are the same activities that have been listed earlier for various other kinds of parent groups.

Keeping in mind the identity need of the parent of today, it hardly seems appropriate to utilize parents for nothing more than serving lunch at school parties. If room mothers are to be selected, they should be deeply involved in the educational program of a given classroom or team area.

Parents' Appreciation Day

Have you ever made a special point of telling parents that you consider it a special privilege to teach their children? Periodically, this should be done. One way is to designate one day each year as *Parents' Appreciation Day.*

Figure 5-5
Mothers and Fathers as Classroom Aides

On this day all parents are invited to school to participate in the operation of the school. Many of the activities that have previously been mentioned as appropriate for American Education Week are also appropriate for this day.

Remember that this day belongs to the parents. Teachers should carefully structure their day so they are free to interact with parents whenever the need arises. This might be a good opportunity for you to show parents that other people can contribute to the teaching act by using children or volunteers to teach. Use whatever classroom gadgets you have to help support instruction on this day.

Following is a sample letter that could be sent home to announce this day:

February 4

Dear Parents:

At a recent meeting of the J. Nelson Kelly PTA executive board, it was decided that a typical PTA meeting would not be appropriate this month. Instead we decided to have a special day for parents. We want to say Thank You for sending your children to school. We have decided to name this day *Kelly Parents' Appreciation Day.* It will be held all day on Wednesday, February 10th.

On this day, and any other for that matter, you are invited to visit school. We hope you will find special interest in the projects that have been made in your honor. After you have seen all you wish, you are invited to stay for refreshments.

What will you see when you come to school? If you arrive any time during the morning you will see language arts and mathematics in most areas. If you come in the afternoon, you are likely to see a variety of things. Rhythms will be taught in the gymnasium all afternoon. You will see science, social studies, music or art if you visit classrooms in the afternoon. From 3:00 p.m. until 3:30 p.m. you will see our recently implemented student tutor program.

We know that all of you are very busy. We also know that it is especially difficult for fathers to get away from work. If you can't come on this day, remember that we are looking forward to your visit any time.

Sincerely,
Kelly Staff

Figure 5-6

Parents' Nights

It is assumed that all schools open their doors to such things as scout groups, homeowners clubs or community agencies that might wish to use the school. However, parents' nights are one dimension of school utilization that has probably not been utilized to any great degree.

The parents of all schools should feel free to use the school facility on a scheduled basis during the year.

At the beginning of the year, via the school Helpbook, send each family a schedule of the parents' nights at the school. Ask two or three interested parents to form a committee to help structure these nights, take charge of the building, and clean up after the evening is over.

There may be many ways that parents wish to use these evenings. They may prefer to have quiet activities in the school library, or they may want to have active things such as team sports, exercise groups or crafts in the gymnasium. Sometimes they may wish to come alone. Other times they may want to participate in these activities with their children.

What they do is not important. What is important is that the school staff have the attitude of sharing the school building and its contents with parents.

Community Resource File

As soon after school begins as possible, each classroom or team area should survey their parents. This will give the teacher ready access to many enriching supplementary activities.

Classroom files have been found to have the advantage of providing the teachers with resources with which they are familiar. If a parent and the teacher have rapport with each other, the use of community resources will be much easier.

School resource files have the advantage of making accessible to the teacher far more resources, but the lack of familiarity with the parents and the problems of coordinating the file might prove to be an obstacle to its use.

Of course, this is not to say that teachers should not seek community resources from every source possible. Cities, rural areas, and university communities are particularly rich in resource people.

Creative Dance

Community Resources
Figure 5-7

An Expert on Eskimos

Sample Survey

Community Resources

Name_____ Address_____

Occupation_____ Phone_____

Yes No   Are you willing to assist in the educational program of our classroom?
         If yes, please check those areas that interest you most.

____Reading	____Knitting	____Cooking
____Science	____Sewing	____Art
____Social Studies	____Typing	____Supervisor on Trips
____Mathematics	____Carpentry	
____Music	____Woodworking	____Clerical Work
____Storytelling	____Weaving	____Gathering Materials
____Dramatics	____Mechanics	
____Supervising Students	____Dance	____Tutoring Children
		____Physical Education
		____Other (Please List)

. . . .

Please Circle Response:

What day of the week is most convenient?   M T W Th   F

What time of the day is most convenient?   AM   PM

Do you need a babysitter?   YES NO

Do you play a musical instrument?   YES NO

List:_____

Do you have hobbies that you would like to share?   YES NO

List:_____

Have you traveled to other states or countries?   YES NO

List:_____

Do you have slides, filmstrips, pictures or other educational materials about
    your travels?   YES NO

List:_____

Do you know of other resource persons in _____ that could contribute to our
    classroom?   YES NO

List:_____

Would you rather work for our classroom in your home?   YES   NO

_____Cooking   _____Repairing Things   _____Mending Books

_____Arranging Trips   _____Typing   _____Other

List:_____

Thank you so much for your consideration in this matter. Our class will be interested in hearing from you.

_____

(Teacher)

Figure 5-8

This survey form is reprinted by permission of the author, Doris Onstad, primary teacher, West School, Grand Forks, North Dakota.

Individualized Field Trips

In this day of great educational activity and the renewed interest in the school as a concept rather than a place, there is a need to rethink the utilization of field trips.

The common use of field trips is to take the entire class to visit something of interest in the city. Sometimes it is correlated with what is taking place in the classroom, and sometimes it has little or nothing to do with classroom activities.

As concepts such as the open classroom, learning centers and the thematic approach to instruction become more commonplace, there is going to be a greater need to individualize field trips.

How can this be done? First, there should be a field trip committee in each school. Requests for a trip should be made through this committee. A teacher might have five children who *need* to go to the public library or a museum because of some project they are pursuing. It would be the responsibility of the committee to make the arrangements, provide the transportation, and in some cases be responsible for supervision of the children. At other times the teacher would accompany the children and parents, teacher aides, or the school principal take the teacher's place in the classroom.

At the beginning of the year all parents should be sent a letter requesting permission to go on field trips. This will save the teacher from having to send home permission letters each time a group plans a trip.

Sample Field Trip Letter

September 15

Dear Parents,

An important part of your child's education is that of taking field trips to various places in and around the community. It has been traditional to send home permission slips each time a trip occurs. Because of the increased frequency of these trips, we would like to get your permission just one time for the entire year.

There are so many varieties of trips that are taken by the children. Sometimes we go out of the city, and sometimes we go two blocks away. Sending home a permission slip with every child each time a trip occurs seems a needless waste of time.

Following are some of the places that children go during the year:

A. Tufte Manor

B. Walks around the school area

C. Various places of business in the city

D. Athletic trips around the city

E. University plays, University library

F. City library

G. Trips outside the city. (Any time a trip outside the city is planned you will be contacted.)

If you feel as though you can give your permission one time for all of these events, please indicate on the space provided. If you feel as though you would like to be contacted each time, please indicate that on the space provided.

· ·

(Tear off and return to Kelly School)

1. ____I give my permission to have my child attend any activities off the school ground. (I understand that I will be contacted when trips outside the city are planned.)

2. ____I wish for my child's teacher to contact me each time a trip is taken.

Name of Child_____

Name of Parent_____

Thank you so much for filling this out and returning it to the school. I hope you feel free to check either of the alternatives.

When a trip is taken we will simply separate the slips and contact those who wish to be contacted.

Sincerely,

Jerry L. Abbott
Principal

Figure 5-9

Liability

The main deterrent to a better use of field trips is that of liability. It may be well to check out the laws of your state before embarking upon an extensive use of individualized field trips as outlined here. In some cases there may be insurance coverage while riding in a school vehicle and not while riding in a parent's vehicle. In cases where transporting children with a parent's vehicle is not allowed, the school PTA might consider subsidizing this program by paying for bus rental, or purchase a school vehicle that could be used for this purpose.

Community Involvement and Time Wasters

There are many times during the course of a school year when teachers just waste time because of the anticipation of some special event. All school holidays are examples. Anyone who has taught elementary age children knows how difficult it is to find meaningful things to do prior to Halloween or Christmas.

This is a good time to use parents in a more meaningful way than pouring kool-aid at the party. One team of teachers, displeased with the way they were using this time, decided to do something different. They invited ten mothers to visit with them after school prior to Halloween day. They asked them if they would help set up stations that children could work at during the entire afternoon. The parents agreed, and this is what happened:

Unknown to the children, ten mothers came to school during the noon hour and set up all the needed paraphernalia for the centers. Needless to say, the children were most excited when they came in from noon break.

The centers were:

Pencil Shavings and Paint
Puppets

Figure 5-10
Community Involvement and Time Wasters

Scrap Material Scarecrows
Pine Cones
Egg Cartons
Crayon Resist
Burlap
Mobiles and Sawdust

At the end of the circuit each child was to have a "Wolfzanger." (sandwich)

The students never worked harder prior to a school party. They worked at many of the centers and made enough projects to share with nearly every teacher in the building, the school library and the halls.

Several positive things resulted from this project. Among them were:

1. It changed the emphasis from one of wasting time while waiting for a school party to one of meaningful involvement.
2. It produced projects that added to the atmosphere of the school.
3. Puppets were made and distributed to the primary rooms for instructional purposes.
4. It allowed teachers to withdraw from the activities and participate in team planning.
5. Involving ten mothers further promoted the partnership between the home and the school.
6. It was an open-ended activity that provided a cohesive feeling between staff and students.
7. Everybody had fun.

PTA and Community Involvement

What is PTA? Is it a meeting each month of the school year where a few parents and a lot of teachers come together for the common good of children? Or is it an ongoing involvement of the school staff with parents for the mutual benefit of all concerned? Hopefully, it is the latter.

Each school should certainly have a parent-teacher association. It should also have a strong program of involvement. One without the other is sure to fail.

It is recommended that the principal work closely with the executive board of the PTA to insure a sound program of activities for the year. It might also be wise to pick a theme for the year and have programs (not too many) suitable to promote that theme. Then, too, there are many instances when it is worthwhile to have an organized effort to get things accomplished. Examples are bond issues, tax levies, a city-wide curricular problem such as family living, or in short a vehicle for promoting massive support for some issue.

Note that in previous sections of this chapter there have been several times when the PTA was used as the sponsoring agency for some of the programs. This is another good reason to have a strong PTA. When you need their structure, you have it.

Never underestimate the power of the parent-teacher association. It will always be a powerful way to bring parents, teachers and children together.

Evaluating Community Involvement

Your school has a strong program of community involvement. How do you know that? Should you note the change in number and intensity of irate phone calls that come from parents? Maybe there has been a change in the amount of conflict between parents and teachers? Maybe the feedback you hear from parents and children about a given classroom or team room indicates that they have been doing a good job of involving parents? These are, of course, indicators of the effectiveness of the program. However, more objective measures are also needed.

Surveys

Surveys are one way of sampling parent attitudes about the school. These surveys can be homemade surveys or they can be patterned after someone like George Gallup, who is expert in the use of surveys. Each year Gallup polls attitudes of parents about the public school. Use his questions, slightly changed to meet your needs, and find out what parents are thinking about the school.

Studies

Oftentimes students and university professors make studies about the involvement of parents in the school program. One such study was recently undertaken by Dr. Sheldon Schmidt, professor at the University of North Dakota. He was trying to find out if there was any correlation between parent involvement in the schools and reading achievement. His study focused on ninety-six Intermediate Four students who were identified through a reading interest test to have little interest in reading. After some instruction in techniques that could be used to help children change their attitudes toward reading, twenty-four parents were assigned to work with one group of children, eight teachers to work with another group, and twenty-four parents and eight teachers to work with another group. The gains made in the third group of children outstripped those made in each of the other groups. The most significant finding was that girls responded well to any of the attempts made to increase their commitment to reading, while the boys made positive gains only when the teacher and the parent worked together.[3]

Schaefer, in an article entitled "Toward a Revolution in Education: A Perspective From Child Development Research," reports the following about parental involvement in the schools:

> The amount of parental involvement in the child's education may explain up to four times as much of the variance in the child's intelligence and achievement test scores at age 11 as the quality of the schools. Douglas, in a national sample of 5,000 children in England, found that parent interest and involvement with the child's education were far more important than the quality of schools, even after statistically controlling for family socioeconomic status.[4]

Feedback

One of the best ways to determine the quality of your program is to constantly ask for feedback from parents, children and staff. Give staff members time, both individually and in meetings, to present what they have concerns about and what they feel good about. Ask the children how they feel about their parents working at the school. This can be done directly, or indirectly through class meetings. Parents who work in the school will be anxious to

---

[3]Sheldon Schmidt, "Reading Growth and Parent Involvement," *Insights,* January-February, 1970, p. 10.

[4]Earl Schaefer, "Toward a Revolution in Education: A Perspective From Child Development Research," *National Elementary Principal,* Vol. LI, Number 1, September, 1971, p. 19.

feedback their feelings about the program of community involvement. Periodic informal gatherings of volunteers is a good technique to use.

Summary

Will parents become this involved in the school? Yes, they will if we let them. Will teachers become involved with parents? Yes, if they feel good about working with other adults and if they receive the proper support from their supervisors.

More than ever before, parents are searching for tasks that fulfill identity needs. One only needs to read the literature of the day to see the great increase of volunteer activities. Why is that? One commonly held idea is that modern housewives live in a technological world and have time on their hands. This is no doubt a factor. People have far more leisure time than they did a few years ago.

But this is only part of the reason. Prior to about 1950 we lived in a survival world. In the survival world people placed goals before roles. They tended to seek goal first, and if anything was left, they gave it to role. Since 1950 that has completely turned around. People born since 1950 place role first. They seek goals only after finding satisfaction in role. This more than anything is causing the mushroom of parents eager to help teachers educate their children. As educators we simply cannot afford to pass up this great opportunity.

Community involvement is a new frontier in education. Almost anything tried is an experiment, since research is lacking. Parents may not know the findings of research; they simply have hunches based upon observation. The time to begin a program of community involvement is now.

Community Involvement IDEA Bank

1. Parents are currently exhibiting a great interest in the school. Poll your parents and find out what they are currently interested in learning. Family Living, Contract Teaching, Open Education, Computer Assisted Instruction, Flexible-Modular Scheduling, and Differentiated Staffing are sure to have high priority. Make small circles of chairs in the gym and

secure a large sign to identify each group. Ask educators and lay people to act as group leaders. Have thirty minutes of discussion about each of the topics. At the end of the thirty minutes ask the group leaders to report to the total group. Use this discussion to help determine direction of the school program.

2. Scan the newspaper each day for items pertaining to your parents. When you find something noteworthy, send them a Good News Letter.

3. Make tape recordings or video tapes of resource persons who work in your school. Place them in a learning station so children can listen again.

4. Keep records of the activities of volunteer workers. Report to them, to the staff, and to the rest of the parents periodically.

5. Organize a parents panel around a topic of current interest, such as poverty, drugs, ecology or race. Ask them to give brief presentations relating to their specialty and follow with discussion. Devote the next meeting to developing skills in dealing with these problems. There are currently several good commercial programs that teach listening. Select one of them to help build these skills in your parents. (Note: The NEA has published a very interesting program, entitled *How to Listen to Your Child and How to Get Your Child to Listen to You.* It contains a study guide, filmstrip and record.)

6. Listening can further be developed by securing a film called *Yellow Summer* from the Iowa Congress of Parents and Teachers. The film is accompanied by a study guide.

7. Parents appreciate a teacher's concern for their child or any member of their family. As soon as you hear that one of the members of the family has entered a hospital, send them a card and follow that up with a visit.

8. Using one of the prepared stencils from the NEA or one of your own, write a fancy letter to your parents requesting them to visit during American Education Week.

9. At the beginning of the school year form several working committees. Some examples could be: Life Time Sports Committee, Field Trips Committee, Educational Supplies Committee and Learning Center Committee. Form the committees around the school program.

10. During the opening days of school, talk with your children about plans for the year. Ask them what they would like to do. Together, come up with a list and call it *Projecting the*

Long Range Goals. Parents will appreciate knowing what you will be studying.

11. Help teachers implement a more relevant, open-ended program for children. This alone will give parents a good feeling about helping in the school. It will also make them see that the new way is more difficult and more help is needed.

12. Develop a Scrounging Committee. It will be their job to gather everything they can find and stockpile it for the school. Wood, cloth, small engines, buttons, leather, paint and magazines are examples of the items necessary to have a good school program.

13. Have parents dress up in costumes and visit school during special days. This can be an ice breaker for community involvement activities.

14. Organize a parents committee around books. This committee will organize a bookstore, order paperback books, take children to the city library, and in general make books more accessible to children.

15. Allow parents with small children a chance to help in school. Sometimes mothers will share babysitting when involved in working at the school. Sometimes mothers want to help but can't come to the school. Send work home with them.

16. Set up a plan whereby parents who have their first child entering your school next year can get information about the school. Set up a buddy plan with neighbors so they will get the desired information about the school.

17. Seek out agencies near the school that can benefit from involvement with children. Homes for the aged, hospitals, crippled children's homes and blind schools are examples. These agencies can be used to develop caring attitudes in children. They can also be an opportunity for children to practice various communication skills. Try to keep the relationship unbroken throughout the year.

18. Invite your parents in for the purpose of showing them how they might contribute to the school program. Structure a number of activities and demonstrate by role playing how the parents might be involved.

19. Have a workshop on cardboard carpentry. Involve the parents by having them make things for your room. Use this as a springboard for other involvement.

20. Try to arrange for a parents' workshop in someone's home. It might be a good way to talk with parents about the school.

21. Have a *Spring Round-up* for your kindergarten parents. Use it both as a way to thank this year's parents for working with you, and as a device to welcome next year's parents. The latter group could be given a brief orientation, followed by a tour of the school. Their children could be taken to the room and shown some of the things they will be doing next year. You could even enrich this experience by having them spend a day in school prior to enrollment. Ask some of the parent volunteers to tell about their work in your classroom.

22. Organize a variety show involving both parents and faculty. You could either charge admission or ask people to make monetary requests for certain numbers on the program. The money could be used to purchase items for the school. This is a great device for developing cohesiveness between parents and teachers.

23. As part of your PTA activities, organize a committee to handle the supervision of the playground during the noon hour. One person is the chairman and responsible for arranging people to be on the playground each day. For each day they miss they must put $2.00 in the *kitty*. The money is used for school supplies, or a *parent-teacher blast* at the end of the year.

24. Each week select a *Child of the Week*. A special bulletin board could be put up in his honor. He is given certain privileges during the week, one of which is to make his parents *Parents of the Week* and invite them to school. They are given a tour of the school, handouts of what the school is doing, and then involved in the child's classroom. At the end of the day both parents and child have an informal chat with the teacher.

25. Begin a Career Awareness Program. Ask certain members of the business community to come in and talk about their work. Then assign a portion of your class to work in their place of business for a couple of hours per day, two or three times per week. This cooperative arrangement will provide both career awareness and involvement by a group that is rarely involved. Members of the business community, although small in number, represent considerable influence in school affairs in most communities.

26. On a given day, have the children come to school at 1:00 p.m. instead of the normal 9:00 a.m. Let school out at 7:00 p.m. This will allow fathers to participate in the school day. If

your class is having experience with cooking in the classroom, they might make a snack for both parents and students.

27. Parents appreciate small things you do for children. If a child is having trouble, invite him back to school some evening or Saturday morning. Both he and his parents will build a cohesive bond with you.

28. Some Intermediate Six teachers continue to work with their students even though they have gone on to junior high school. This, too, will build a cohesive bond with parents.

29. Take a day occasionally and invite all of your parents to come and view the program. Prepare for them by planning activities that both show them what is taking place in the school and directly involve them in the classroom. Children's programs, displays, talk sessions with parents after school, etc., are all good devices to use during this special day.

30. Parents feel good about coming to school if you can find a way to involve them directly in the activities of the classroom. One way is to send home a note asking each parent to participate in a project that will help their child's reading. Each child will record a tape. His parents come to the classroom during the reading period and together they make a tape of the child's reading, using a basal reader. A basal reader is suggested because skills are arranged sequentially and each can have access to the same story. The tape is then played back and together the child and the parent note the oral reading errors. A discussion of the child's reading follows. Cards should be made available to each parent with the following oral reading skills on them:

   A. Correct Phrasing
   B. Voice Inflection
   C. Quality of Tone
   D. Pronunciation
   E. Enunciation
   F. Skipping Words or Lines
   G. Word Substitution
   H. Addition of Words
   I. Ignores Word Errors
   J. Repetition of Words
   K. Observes Punctuation

   (In most cases the parents will not be familiar with the above skills. There should be a definition of each skill on the back of the card. In some school communities it might be necessary to have in-service training to adequately use this technique.)

31. Invite parents in for the purpose of seeking direction for your community involvement program. Following are some *starters* to get good interaction:
    A. How can we improve the program?
    B. What do you have concerns about?
    C. What do you feel good about?
    D. Do you feel better about the school now that you are involved?
    E. Have you found a way to make input into the school program in terms of helping to effect decision making?
    F. Can untrained people work in the classroom and make a contribution?
    G. Do you feel your involvement has made it easier to confront the teacher when you have a concern?
    H. What other areas of community involvement could be investigated?
    I. How could our training sessions be improved?
    J. How are your children reacting to your involvement in the school?
    K. Do you think it is generally understood what it is we are trying to accomplish?
    L. Are the teachers enthusiastic about your work in their classrooms?
    M. Are there various degrees of involvement so you have a choice about what you want to do?
32. One of the best ways to improve community understanding is to send home a happy child each night. Take some time during the school day to summarize the day's activities. Remind the children to talk to their parents about what they do in school. Of course, it will help if the children have some physical evidence of having accomplished something–projects, papers, books, etc.
33. Make every effort to have the regular teaching staff interact with parent volunteers. They should know their names and visit with them when the opportunity presents itself. Parent volunteers, like any other staff members, need to know they are making a contribution.
34. It is becoming more common to connect federal funding with community involvement. If your school is involved in programs such as Headstart and Title I, set up an advisory committee of parents to help coordinate the program.
35. Some schools have an *Ease Into Monday* program organized for the purpose of giving teachers some time together to plan for the week's activities and allowing children to begin the

week with a good feeling about school. Survey your parents to find any of them who may wish to participate by making a presentation of some sort to the children. Music, plays, slides, films, and projects are examples of some of the things they could do. Schedule them several weeks in advance so they know when it is their turn.

36. Because of the current interest in hobbies, crafts, sewing, knitting, cooking, etc., and because they almost require a cooperative relationship with parents, use them as a way to more deeply involve parents. For example, cooking in the classroom is a very worthwhile activity. Invite some parents to participate by actually working with the children. Others may wish to be involved to the extent that they will send the ingredients. Give all parents feedback on projects such as these and stress how you coordinate these activities with classroom objectives. During a unit in cooking you could give parents the following positive data:

 A. Cooking activities help students develop group cohesiveness.

 B. Cooking requires children to follow directions.

 C. Cooking requires careful reading.

 D. Cooking calls upon the child's mathematical skills.

 E. Cooking requires that each child be responsible for bringing the specific ingredients. Failure to do so influences the end product.

37. Use every opportunity possible to send communication upward. For instance, if your school has a severe problem such as busing, boundary changes, overcrowding, etc., do not wait for someone else to solve your problem. Use your parent-teacher association to study the problem and send their own recommendation to the school board. This is not to say that your school will always get its way. However, your effort will be one more input into the problem solving process—and, of course, it is easier to live with a decision you helped to influence.

38. Force is rarely recommended as a technique to elicit change. Sometimes, for a variety of reasons such as boundary changes, bond issues, and tax levies, it might be necessary. Be ready on these occasions by having a calling committee. Select one member of the PTA to be chairman of this committee. Use your room mothers as the contact people. When trouble arises, the chairman calls on two or three room mothers, who

in turn call the parents of each class. In a few minutes you can have your complete parent group at a meeting that may have pronounced effect upon your school.

39. Sometimes it is difficult to get people to attend meetings. Use the following techniques to increase attendance:
   A. Provide baby sitters.
   B. Hold meetings in the afternoons.
   C. Sometimes people fear the school. Hold some of your meetings in places that appear more friendly to these people.
   D. Provide transportation.
   E. Have warm, friendly meetings that are over in fifty minutes.
   F. Use nametags to develop group cohesiveness.

40. Many school systems have adopted *Management by Objective.* This is an accountability system that calls for: (1) deciding what it is you want to happen in your school, (2) writing specific objectives for everything in your school, (3) implementing the various objectives, and (4) evaluating how well each objective was met. At the beginning of each year, try to formulate a statement of goals for community involvement. Under each broad goal statement, write specific objectives. Present it to your staff. Ask them to use your statement to make one of their own. Explain to them that writing things down will make these objectives more achievable. Below is a sample of how a statement might look:

Goal Number One: Community Involvement

Statement: With rapid educational change comes parental concern. If not checked, this concern can lead to rebellion. Therefore, it is my intention to have a program of community involvement that allows parents first-hand information and involvement in their child's education. I will do the following:

___1. I will meet with all new parents before school opens.
___2. I will send a Kelly Helpbook to each parent near the beginning of the school year.
___3. I will send home a newsletter in the middle of each reporting period.
___4. I will cooperatively plan with my staff activities for American Education Week.
___5. I will organize a Kelly Parents' Appreciation Day.

___6. I will use the Good News Slips to better relate to parents.

___7. I will work closely with the PTA Executive Committee to assure meaningful PTA activities. We will have a minimum of six meetings for parents and six meetings of the board.

___8. I will keep parents informed of all changes in school routine.

___9. I will meet with the staff and cooperatively draft a plan for community involvement activities for this school year. I will support all efforts to implement this plan.

41. What single activity could you have that: (1) deeply involves nearly all of your parents, (2) earns money for the school, (3) children look forward to with great anticipation, (4) produces a sense of cooperation and mutual respect among parents, teachers and children? Of course, the school carnival. Have one each year and see how parents and children begin to look forward to this opportunity to interact with you in a way that seems difficult with many other activities.

42. Teachers should be generous in their use of Good News Letters. These letters need not always be on paper. Sometimes it might be nice to send a tape player and cassette home with a Good News report.

43. Have each student in your class adopt a *grandparent* from a neighboring nursing home. Ask them to make contact at least once every two weeks. Deep involvement with the aged can be very beneficial both to the grandparent and to the child.

44. At the end of the school year send a *Things To Do* letter home with each child. Emphasize activities that parents and children can do together. Following is a sample letter that could be used:

A Things To Do List For Vacation

Dear Children and Parents,

For most children, three months of vacation is too long. Following is a list of activities that parents and children can enjoy together:

1. Collecting:

   Make a collection of something that is available in quantity and variety. Some examples could be rocks, seeds, leaves, fabrics, baseball cards, paper, bottles, and buttons. Use the collection for a study of color, texture, classification, etc.

2. Scrapbook:

Keep a scrapbook of pictures of something that you are interested in, such as pets, boats, athletes, airplanes, designs or flowers.

3. Family Bulletin Board:

Be responsible for a family bulletin board. Make it from a piece of corrugated paper from a box. Post family reminders on it. Write announcements, newsletters, and funny things that have happened to you or members of your family.

4. Science Walk:

Go on a science walk by yourself or with a member of the family. Try to make at least one new discovery on each walk. Take a notebook along and make lists of insects, trees, etc. This will also be a good technique to add to your collections.

5. Diary:

Keep a diary of things that happened to you over the summer. Your friends and classmates at school will enjoy reading about your activities.

6. Learn Something New:

Commit yourself to learning something new each day. Prepare a salad or a dessert for dinner, sew a button on a jacket, arrange flowers for the table, teach your pet a new trick, read a news article and report to your family, or paint the fence.

7. Reading:

Plan to do some reading each day. Sometimes you could read to yourself and sometimes your parents or other family members could read to you. Occasionally prepare something so well that you read it aloud to members of your family.

8. Writing:

Write in a journal each day. Write plays based on the stories in the *Summer Weekly Reader* or *Highlights for Children.* Write thank you notes for parties, picnics, gifts and courtesies received.

9. Arts and Crafts:

Paint, sketch, weave, model clay, play an instrument. Learn a poem, make puppets and give a puppet show for your friends. Make litterbags, picturebooks, or discarded greeting card scrapbooks for children in hospitals.

10. Travel:
    The key to travel is observation. Take your journal and diary along on all trips. Note such things as highways, kinds of cars, different methods of farming, farm products, and rock formations.

This is just a beginning. How many new ideas can you add?

                          Have fun,
                          Mrs. Ferrie
                          Mrs. Quale

45. There is a growing concern about children who are not exposed to good books. Programs such as *Reading is Fundamental* are springing up all over the nation. Paperback books are purchased in great numbers by PTAs and civic groups and bussed around to various centers. It takes a lot of parental participation to make these programs a success. Try it in your community. It may just be the spark that is needed to produce a more cooperative relationship between parents and the school staff.

46. Current research indicates there is little value in the typical substitute teaching arrangement. Change the focus of substitutes by asking each of them to prepare a half-day presentation on something that *turns them on* and *turns the children on.* It may be a hobby, a skill they possess, or some facet of their work. The remainder of the day is devoted to those activities planned by the classroom teacher or teachers. The teacher selects the substitute on the basis of the appropriateness of the presentation as well as traditional selection procedures.

47. Invite parents in and discuss the many ways they might contribute to your classroom. Go around the room and ask each parent what they would feel good about sharing. One group of parents gave the following responses: sewing, knitting, cooking, cake decorating, handyman, carpentry, beekeeping, music, sports, story telling, drama, dance, camping, painting, art work, antiquing furniture, and flower arranging.

48. A good way to build a cohesive bond between parents and the school is to have an all-school picnic the first week of school. The picnic is held on the school grounds and the agenda can be formal or informal.

49. Write a letter to all of your parents during the first few days of school. In the first paragraph say a few things about

yourself, in the second talk about your plans for the year, and in the third invite parental participation.

50. Many schools send home a calendar of events for the year. Use an early art period to make a creative calendar for each family. Emphasize the idea that the more eye catching they make it, the better chance their parents will have of remembering the events.

51. Most parent-teacher associations have a thirty minute period prior to their meetings for room visitations. Use this time as a training session for parents who wish to work in the classroom. Those not involved can either observe the training sessions or view things of interest in the classroom.

52. Parents will become more actively involved in your school if you go out of your way to help their children. An ever-present problem is that of Intermediate Sixth students adjusting to junior high school. Instead of the typical presentation by the counselor, use this three-step approach: (1) Buddy team all of your students with a student from the junior high school and have them follow him through a morning. (2) Invite junior high students to come to your school and act as group leaders for a small group discussion on what they observed during their visit. (3) Ask the counselor to make a presentation about the junior high school.

53. Write a letter to your class prior to the opening of school. Build investment with them by giving some insight into the excitement that will be theirs once school begins.

54. One of the most controversial subjects in all of education is that of busing students to obtain equality of educational opportunity. The alternative, say the opponents, is not to maintain racial balance through busing, but rather to make every school a quality school. One way this can be achieved is to "bus" parents instead of children. Parents from inner city areas become volunteers in suburban centers, and parents from suburban areas become volunteers in inner city centers. The result is a lot of worthwhile work being done in the schools by parents, and a data base upon which to decide the best alternatives to quality education for every child in America.

55. It is a rare elementary school which gives art adequate time in its curriculum. If you want both to accomplish something in the area of art and at the same time involve members of your community, begin a Picture Lady Program. Each school

purchases about $100 worth of pictures. Volunteer mothers, all trained in the program, come to the school on a scheduled basis and instruct various classes. The pictures stay in each school for a period of time and are then rotated to other schools in the district.

56. Parents are anxious to get direct, timely information about their child's reading program. Using the form below or one of your own, report reading progress to parents and use them as a unique resource to analyze their child's progress.

```
                                    _____
                                              (Date)
   _____ has read _____ to me.

                                    _____
                                              Teacher
Comments: _____

   _____

   _____

                                    _____
                                              Parents
```

57. Do you have children that you aren't deeply enough involved with to get the kind of commitment you want from them? If so, take note of the extra curricular activities they are involved in and take some time to watch them participate. You will be surprised how rapidly commitment will come after you have seen a child participate in a park board hockey game, a YMCA basketball game, or attended a musical event in which he took part.

58. Community involvement is just one of the many activities that infringe upon a teacher's time. If this is not kept in steady focus, the program could dissipate. Take a calendar from either the "Grade Teacher" or the "Instructor" and note all of the highlights for the month. Use them as springboards for community involvement. For instance, during National Diabetes Week you might invite a doctor to come in and talk about diabetes, insulin or how to treat children who are in insulin shock. During Negro History Week you might invite someone to come in and talk about the

accomplishments of black Americans. On days which aren't particularily significant, you might write in activities such as: Send home a Good News Letter, invite your parents to visit school, or take three children to the city library today. You will be surprised how easy it will be to keep a steady focus on community involvement.

59. One of the best ways to determine the effectiveness of your reading program is to check both the quantity and quality of children's writing. Establish a parents committee on creative writing. Each teacher sends creative writings to the committee. They edit them, and produce a city-wide creative writing booklet that is distributed three or four times per year. This can be made more interesting by involving parents in workshops to stimulate children's writing.

60. Together with your staff and some interested parents, make a list of what to look for in a visit to your school. Make the list positive and available to all who visit. It could also be a page in your school Helpbook.

61. Invite your parents to accompany their children to school on a given morning for breakfast. Parents, children and teacher(s) use this time to freely interact in a stress-free climate. Making the fathers responsible for the breakfast could be an interesting way to get them involved.

62. Parents who work actively in the school should be encouraged to meet periodically and share their concerns and good feelings about their activities. These ideas should be written down and used as orientation materials for future parents who wish to become involved in the school but aren't sure what they can do.

63. If you have a sound program of community involvement, you have already sampled the competencies of your parents. Find a father who could give helpful hints to other fathers about such things as: how to panel a basement, how to do estate planning, how to lay bricks, how to do organic gardening, how to save money on your income tax, or a host of other things related to saving both time and money. After the presentation, arrange activities that will provide for more interaction between the men on the staff and the fathers of the neighborhood.

Chapter 6

Parents as Partners: Reporting Pupil Progress

Few practices in school are more demeaning, degrading, and destructive than that of giving grades to elementary children. Instead of fulfilling the intended purpose of reporting pupil progress and keeping close ties with parents, they report almost nothing of value and, in many cases, contribute to the unfriendliness of schools.[1]

Time and time again this position has been supported by research. One of the most recent affirmations of the destructiveness of the prevailing reporting system was made by Arlene Silberman. Her conclusion after a seven month study of two hundred and seventy-one report cards was: Most report cards are failing. They fail to tell mothers and fathers what they need to know about their children.[2]

Dr. William Glasser, eminent psychiatrist and author of several books on the subject of how people deal with self, has concluded

---

[1]Sidney Simon, "Alternatives to Grading" (Amherst, Mass.: University of Mass.), p. 1.

[2]Arlene Silberman, "How Report Cards Can Harm Children and Mislead Parents" (New York, N.Y.: Downe Publishing, Inc.: *Ladies Home Journal,* March, 1972), p. 74.

that there is a high positive correlation between school failure and failure in life, and that present practice has absolutely no utility in the present society.

The Present Society

Since about 1950, and that date could be a few years either way, about 500 million people in the Western world rather abruptly shifted from a survival society (goal-role) to an identity society (role-goal).

In the survival society there was a preoccupation with goals. Only if satisfaction was found in goal would one seek role. Youngsters presently in the schools, all born since the shift, are now more concerned about role. Questions like "Who am I?" "Where am I going?" "What can I do for others?" have far more significance to them than the most frequently asked goal questions, "Will I measure up scholastically?" "Where do I fit in the business world?" and "Will I end up a winner or a loser as measured by material wealth?"

Just because people are concerned about role does not mean they will not seek goal. They will seek it enthusiastically, but not at the expense of role.

What does this say about the operation of our schools? It says there is no longer any utility in separating the winners and the losers. There are simply too many losers in that kind of a system. Dr. Glasser says that he has asked many students about what they consider good grades and bad grades. It turns out that just below a B is considered failure.[3] When asked if this means they got a failing grade the answer is invariably no. It means they are a failing person.

And what are the options for a failing person, especially in an identity society? There are none—at least, none that are acceptable. Students who leave school failing have few options but more failure, loneliness, frustration, boredom, unemployment, and perhaps worse. Drugs, crime, and mental hospitals are common havens for the failing person.

Does this mean that children should never fail? Of course not.

---

[3]William Glasser, *Schools Without Failure* (New York, N.Y.: Harper and Row Publishers, Inc., 1969), p. 63.

Failure experience is part of everyone's life. What it means is that no child will leave the schools having had so many failure experiences that they will consider themselves a life-long failure.

So the charge is clear. Educators must examine what they are doing, not only in the way they report to parents, but what they report to parents. If either is causing children to view themselves as failures, action must be taken.

Mrs. Silberman, in her study of nearly three hundred report cards, was struck by the negativeness that seemed to run through so many of the systems. In one school, hopefully the exception rather than the rule, she found the following list under the heading of "Social Development, Work Habits and Attitudes":

> Is discourteous and uncooperative
> Lacks respect for the rights of others
> Finds the work too difficult
> Lacks self-control
> Does not accept responsibility
> Works carelessly
> Wastes time
> Does not follow directions
> Does not complete work on time
> Lacks initiative
> Is inattentive
> Needs to develop good study habits
> Does not work to capacity[4]

Doesn't that make one want to re-examine methods used to report to parents?

Parents Lead the Way

As in so many things, it looks like educators have abdicated their leadership position. It looks like few things will happen to change the system until parents demand it.

On the bright side, increasingly parents are requesting that schools not report to them with the traditional grade card. In my own experience I recently received a letter from a parent which in part reads:

> We are writing this letter in the hope that it may help you influence the board of education in regard to report cards in the

---

[4]Silberman, "How Report Cards Can Harm Children," p. 74.

elementary school. Our first child entered kindergarten this year, and until now we have been more than pleased with the educational philosophy of the teacher and supposedly in a larger sense, the school system. In our opinion, Mrs. McCabe represents the ideal kindergarten teacher. In her classroom there exists freedom with rules and a respect for individuality. She uses learning centers most effectively to preserve that aspect. However, on January 26 the first report card arrived. We believed a reversal of educational philosophy took place in the grading of the card. For the most part, adults do not consider S and N as grades; however, a child who has never been graded A, B, C definitely thinks of S and N as grades, namely, good and poor. They somehow learn this before the first report card.

Isn't it incredible that parents must lead the way when it comes to reporting pupil progress? Why have educators stood in the background on this very vital issue?

Negative Aspects of the Current System

It is well known that some very destructive things happen to children as the result of grades. To review them once more, the use of grades perpetuates the following:

A. Grades set up power struggles between people.
B. Grades tend to accentuate the winners in our society and degrade the losers.
C. Grades encourage cheating.
D. Grades oftentimes support bad teaching.
E. Grades tend to negatively affect human relationships.
F. Grades tend to prolong dependency upon adults.
G. Grades tend to postpone self-evaluation.

Four Step Approach to Reporting Pupil Progress

Why do educators do what they know is wrong? They do it because it is the easy way out. It doesn't take a lot of time or thought to put a few numbers or letters on a card.

It is also done because it supports the kind of teaching they are doing. If every task completed by a child is scored, and these scores averaged, it only seems appropriate, at least to many, that these scores be used to separate the winners and the losers.

Like any other change for the better, more will be required of the entire school staff. This again is another reason for the implementation of an auxiliary program in every school.

Any method of accurately reporting pupil programs must consider more than a report card. Following is a plan that will insure more meaningful communication between the home and the school:

- Teacher Diagnosis
- Released Time for Conferencing
- The Written Report
- Individualized Parent-Teacher Conferences

Teacher Diagnosis

This is the most vital part of reporting pupil progress. Without a good diagnosis, the rest of the process is meaningless. Whenever a teacher or team of teachers makes any kind of contact with parents, he should be prepared to talk about the child in a very specific way. If the problem is social, the teachers should attempt to tell the parents what kinds of processes they are using to help the child overcome his difficulty. They should also be prepared to suggest alternatives that parents might use to help the child. If the problem is curricular, the teachers should have specific knowledge relative to where the child is in the skill sequence and show parents samples of the work that is currently being done. And they should be able to suggest ways the parents can support what is being done in school.

Many schools today have adopted a learning system that identifies the skills to be learned and states a very specific behavioral objective for each skill. Record keeping is usually very specific. This should make it rather easy for the teacher to explain where the child is functioning at any given time.

In schools which do not have as specific a system, the teacher can make folders of the child's work, along with a checklist of skills for each subject. For example, Dr. Walter B. Barbe several years ago made a very detailed reading skills checklist, using all of the available basal readers.[5] They are organized according to age level. When discussing reading, the teacher could bring out this

---

[5]Walter Barbe, *Educator's Guide to Personalized Reading Instruction* (Englewood Cliffs, N.J.: Prentice-Hall, Inc., 1961), pp. 142, 152, 161, 169, 183, 193, 205.

skills checklist, or one of several like it, and explain to the parents exactly what is happening with respect to reading skills.

There are many ways to report specific skills to parents. In general, the more diagnostic the teacher is, the more she has internalized the skills to be taught, and the more successful she will be in reporting pupil progress.

Released Time for Conferencing

Accurate reporting requires commitment from all levels of the educational enterprise. From the teacher is required an accurate assessment of where the child is, and the commitment to report that assessment on a regular basis.

From the school board is required a commitment to reschedule the school day. This can be done in one of several ways. Some schools dismiss one-half day each week for planning and reporting to parents. Others choose to shorten their lunch hours and dismiss early each day. Whatever the plan, there should be regular periods built into the day that provide for ongoing reporting to parents and students.

From the parents there needs to be a commitment to stay in close contact with teachers, and a basic agreement on the importance of using school time for this important activity.

From supervisors is needed the commitment to continually seek ways to refine the system, and at the same time make sure that teachers do not violate the plan. To allow teachers to use the time for things other than the intended purpose would undermine the plan.

Some schools might argue that it isn't possible to use school time for reporting on a regular basis. If they were to examine the number of days they now use for in-service activities, parent-teacher conferences, and numerous other things, they would probably find they would use less instructional time in this plan than they had previously.

The Written Report

There are many techniques that can be used to relate in written form how a child is doing in school. They range from subjective statements about his work to very detailed checklists. Both are probably unacceptable because they represent an ideal which few teachers can achieve.

The not so specific checklist, supported with the other three prongs of this plan, probably represents the most realistic way to make a written report to parents. The very specific checklist is unrealistic and confusing. To relate to a parent how the child applies rules for accenting, or some rule of syllabication, is to only confuse the issue. Yet to say in a checklist that the child reads well is to tell a parent almost nothing about the child's progress in reading. Somewhere in between these poles lies a written report that is both realistic and attainable.

If not carefully constructed, the checklist has the same destructive qualities as the card that reports A, Bc C. In the words of Mark Twain, "The difference between the right word and the almost right word is the difference between the lightning and the lightning bug." Phrases like *accepts responsibility, practices self-control, works neatly,* and *follows directions,* can probably be stated in more positive ways. The emphasis should be upon the child's own individuality, his creativity, and his self concept.

The sample checklist that follows is a compilation of some twenty checklists collected over a period of several years. Because of great differences from school to school, it is suggested that it be used only as a guide for the development of one that meets the needs of a given school.

The Checklist

side #1

Dear Parents:

Individual diagnosis of your child's strengths, weaknesses, interests and styles of learning are so much more important than letter grades on a report card. When these things are known the teacher can better tailor a program to meet the needs of each child.

Because of our commitment to reporting pupil progress in a humane and accurate way, we have devised the following checklist with the hope that it will provide you with more complete information about your child.

We solicit your comments.

Sincerely,

_____

(Director of Elementary Education)

Evaluation of Student Progress: Elementary Report

_____Public Schools

School_____Date_____

Student_____

Teacher(s)_____   _____

_____   _____

Attendance:	1	2	3	4	Total
Days Present:					
Days Absent:					
Times Tardy:					

KEY TO UNDERSTANDING THIS REPORT

Various aspects of each subject area are listed. The teacher(s) will use this report in a way that best meets the needs of the child. The following uses are suggested: (1) If a child is doing as well as he can, as judged by himself and his teacher, ACCEPTABLE PROGRESS will be checked. (2) If the child is not doing as well as he can, as judged by himself and his teacher, AREA WHICH NEEDS WORK will be checked. (3) If the child is doing acceptable work for his judged ability, yet needs work in the area, both will be checked. (4) Sometimes, for various reasons, the teacher may want to report only in specific areas. In that case she may mark DNA (Does Not Apply) in the other areas.

Side #2

Language Arts (reading, spelling, language, listening, writing, oral communication)	Acceptable Progress	Area Which Needs Work	Acceptable Progress	Area Which Needs Work	Acceptable Progress	Area Which Needs Work	Acceptable Progress	Area Which Needs Work
Reads with Comprehension								
Shows Interest in Reading								
Oral Reading								
Applies Reading Skills								
Expression in Writing								
Mechanics in Writing								
Use of Spelling in Written Work								
Listening								
Mathematics								
Numerical Relationships								

Side #2 continued	Acceptable Progress	Area Which Needs Work	Acceptable Progress	Area Which Needs Work	Acceptable Progress	Area Which Needs Work	Acceptable Progress	Area Which Needs Work
Geometric Relationships								
Applies Reasoning in Problem Solving								
Shows Proficiency in Computation								
Social Studies								
Is Learning Basic Concepts								
Contributes to Projects and Discussion								
Uses Reference Materials								
Transfers Fact to Generalization								
Science								
Developing Skill in Manipulation and use of Science Materials								
Participates in Projects and Discussion								
Problem Solving Techniques								
Is Learning Basic Concepts								

Side #3

Physical Education and Health	Acceptable Progress	Area Which Needs Work	Acceptable Progress	Area Which Needs Work	Acceptable Progress	Area Which Needs Work	Acceptable Progress	Area Which Needs Work
Concerned About Personal Health								
Participates in Physical Activities								
Skill Development								
Art								
Shows Interest and Participation in Art								
Growth in Expression								
Skill Development in Art								
Skill in Manipulation of Music Materials								
Music								
Participates in Music Class								
Skill in Manipulation of Music Materials								
Skill Development								
Band								

Side #3 continued	Acceptable Progress	Area Which Needs Work	Acceptable Progress	Area Which Needs Work	Acceptable Progress	Area Which Needs Work	Acceptable Progress	Area Which Needs Work
String								
Toward a Full Development of Self								
Stable Limits (self control)								
Assumes Responsibility (initiative, self direction)								
Creativity (imagination, resourcefulness, inventiveness, curiosity, originality)								
Self Concept (pride, self confidence)								
Desire for Knowledge								
Lifelong Commitment to Learning								
Enthusiasm								
Cooperation (sharing, courtesy)								

Side #4

Comments: (This section is to be used to make any of the general items on the checklist more specific. In general, it is intended to indicate the unique qualities of the child)

_____

                                        Teacher

. . . .

(For parent use only: Feedback Sheet)
I have read the checklist. I desire:

___1. A School Visit (conference)
___2. A Phone Visit
___3. A Home Visit
___4. _____   _____

                                        Parent

Figure 6-1

Individualized Parent-Teacher Conferences

No program of pupil reporting can be complete without considering an alternative to present methods of conferencing. Individualized Parent-Teacher Conferences is such an alternative, and if used properly can give meaning to the entire process of reporting to parents. Five different contacts have been identified. They are:

A. Good News Letter:
   This is sent home with children when something they have done deserves positive reinforcement. Sometimes they are sent to parents who for some reason deserve to be recognized.

_____

Good News Letter

                                        Date_____

Dear_____,
        GOOD NEWS!!!_____

_____

                                        _____

                                        (Teacher)

Figure 6-2

_____

B. School Visit:

This is a very productive contact because it gives parents, teachers and children a chance to interact in an atmosphere where much learning takes place. There should be emphasis upon making the child an important part of the conference.

C. Phone Visit:

Small concerns call for small contacts. This contact is used when a face-to-face visit is not considered necessary. Papers that are not handed in on time, lack of punctuality, or a lost item of clothing might be a reason to use this contact.

D. Home Visit:

The home visit is an excellent way for a partnership to develop between parents and teachers. Teachers should commit themselves to at least one home visit per year with each child. At the first informal gathering with parents at the beginning of the year, reasons for the home visit should be discussed. Walking home with the child at the end of the school day is a good way to break the ice for a home visit. This contact is excellent for developing cohesion with a child and his parents, and allows parents a chance to interact in their own environment.

E. Miscellaneous Visit:

Teachers see parents in many different places. Some are appropriate to discuss children and others are not. Teachers can use this contact to discuss little things that may mean a lot to parents. Of course, the teacher would rarely discuss school progress unless there was some degree of privacy.

Whenever a teacher finds it appropriate to make a contact with parents, a decision must be made about the type of contact. One of the five is chosen, based upon the nature of the concern. When conference time draws near, the teacher studies her records and decides whether or not a conference is necessary. If so, she simply gives the parent's name to the school secretary and a conference is scheduled. If she finds it is unnecessary, she calls the parents and makes her feelings known to them. With their concurrence they do not meet on that occasion, and more time is applied to those parents who wish to consult with the teacher for an extended time.

Individualized Parent-Teacher Conference Sheet

Parent_____

Student_____

_____ Good News Letter

_____ School Visit

_____ Phone Visit

_____ Home Visit

_____ Misc. Visit

Subject:_____   Comments:

Date:_____

M_____ F_____

GNL_____ Phone_____ School_____

Home_____Misc._____

Reason:

Subject:_____   Comments:

Date: _____

M_____ F_____

GNL_____Phone_____School_____

Home_____Misc._____

Reason:

Figure 6-3

This use of conferences has brought about more positive contacts with parents. There has also been a great increase in the number of such contacts. (Note: One year a team of 75 children and three staff members had 460 contacts with parents. Traditionally it would have been less than half that number.)

Reporting to Parents and Team Teaching

This type of reporting is very appropriate when the school is organized around team teaching and differentiated staffing. If the traditional type of conference is used, there may be times when a teacher aide, out of necessity, confers with the parent. This might give parents the impression their child has been assigned to a teacher aide. This should never happen with individualized parent-teacher conferences.

A Lingering Concern

To be effective, schools must be built on trust. A reporting system that does not allow for child input is not evidencing this important characteristic.

It is recommended that children be included in all phases of the reporting plan. When checklists are filled out, the child should be consulted. At times it may be appropriate for him to make a self-evaluation and compare it with the perception of the teacher. When conferences are held with parents, children should be included as often as possible.

Closely related to this is that of continually asking children for feedback. If the school places great emphasis upon the individual conference, there is a provision for built-in feedback sessions. If the school emphasizes group work, efforts need to be made to ask the children for feedback on a regular basis.

Children need to be included in every phase of the classroom. They should be helping to set goals. They should be asked about their concerns, and what they feel good about. They should also be included in the process of reporting pupil progress to parents. Commitment to these simple rules can significantly decrease the incidence of problems related to communicating with the home.

Tips on Conferencing

A good conference does not just happen. Only when teachers begin to understand the relationship between diagnosis and conferencing will parents begin getting the information they want. The following are some tips to insure success in the conference:

Introductions

People rarely function well together unless some time has been taken to develop cohesion. The success of the conference might very well be decided in the opening moments of introduction. Use any technique that works for you to get this investment. Talking about the weather, the child, or some incident that may have meaning for both parties is a good way to get the conference going.

Who Speaks?

There are some good reasons for both parties carrying the conversation. On the one hand, parents come to get data about their child. On the other, they have valuable data that you need to do the best job of teaching. Try not to give too many solutions. It is usually best to lead people into finding their own solutions.

Conference Setting

Conferences can take place in many places: the office, the classroom, or the home. Wherever, place is not as important as the setting. Never sit across from a parent with the desk in between. This is not a psychologically appropriate arrangement.

Diagnosis

Be as diagnostic as possible. Parents want to know what skills are being taught and how well they have been mastered. It would be a mistake to think this is all they are interested in knowing. They also want diagnostic information about peer relationships, self-concept, and a host of other things related to the welfare of the child.

Giving Solutions

After developing some expertise in conferencing the teacher will know when to ask for solutions and when to give them. Too much of either is not appropriate. Teachers should learn the *Self Enhancing Education* technique of Reflective Listening.[6] In reflective listening you try to hear the person at the feeling level. After all of the feelings are out, the reflector tries then to state his feeling condition. Solutions result when the two are put together.

Telling the Nice Things

It is very reinforcing for parents to hear nice things about their children. And teachers are guilty of too often not telling about the good things children do. However, in the conference setting, the teacher should be as honest as possible, and confront parents about problems the child is having. Another *Self Enhancing*

---

[6]Norma Randolph, William Howe and Elizabeth Achterman, *Self Enhancing Education: A Training Manual* (Santa Clara, California, Self Enhancing Education, Inc., 1971), p. 1.

Education technique, called Congruent Forthright Sending Showing Ownership, will help make this confrontation beneficial to the child.[7]

Power Struggles

Do not allow yourself to get into a power struggle with a parent. Reflective listening will keep you out of power struggles.

Confidentiality

It is not appropriate to talk about other children in the conference. Rapport can completely break down as a result of breaking confidence.

Ending the Conference

End the conference on a happy note if at all possible. Do not allow parents to leave until they know what to do to improve the child's progress.

Summary

"The plan sounds good, but parents won't accept it." How often educators have used this as an excuse for not doing something.

Recently, our school system experimented with the use of conferences and checklists as an alternative to sending home an A, B, C report card. To our astonishment, parents were overwhelmingly in favor of abolishing the present system.

There are 6,500 elementary children in the Grand Forks Public Schools. Of that total, about 60 per cent were surveyed at the same time they conferenced with the teacher. The response in favor of conferences and checklists instead of the A, B, C report card ranged from 75 to 85 per cent in the fourteen schools. Could you find greater consensus on any issue?

It has often been said that the reporting system of a school mirrors its value system. Every time we send home a report to parents we are saying something about our school. How much longer are we going to let that value system be represented by A . . . B . . . C . . . ?

---

[7] Randolph, Howe and Achterman, *SEE Training Manual*, p. 1.

Chapter 7

Effective Activities for Auxiliaries to Use with Children

It has been established that auxiliaries can make significant contributions to schools. The variety of talent they bring to the school setting staggers the imagination. However, talent is not enough. There must also be a constant flow of creative ideas to properly exploit that talent. The challenge to the professional staff is to develop effective activities at a rate proportional to the needs of the auxiliary team.

The last several years have witnessed a gradual shift from the single textbook approach to one of individualized programs. Hardly a day goes by without some new *package* being rolled off the press.

These new educational programs have made lasting contributions toward the motivation of children in school. The effective teacher has the ability to utilize these things in such a way as to bring them all together into a meaningful whole.

The *super-creative teacher* can do this and more. She also takes the things of the environment and uses them to stimulate children to do better in school. The use of catalogs to teach reading, assembling model cars to teach following directions, and cooking in the classroom to teach mathematical concepts are some examples of what creative teachers are doing to stimulate children.

One teacher was dissatisfied with the way he was teaching critical reading. The worksheets he was using just weren't doing the job. One day he came into the classroom with a cereal box top. He told the children that a company had an unusual offer to all who used their product, and wondered if they would like to send for it. The box top advertised a submarine. He carefully read all of the advertisement and then asked for a show of hands. Of course all of the children were excited about this unusual offer. After several weeks the submarine arrived. The teacher opened it up, looked at it, and put it in his desk. He then told the children about the arrival of the submarine and asked them some questions about what they thought they had purchased. Of course there was a tremendous discrepancy between what they had purchased and what they thought they had purchased. They all had a good laugh and the teacher had taught a lasting lesson on critical reading. He had hooked their interest as a result of utilizing the experiential level of the children.

One of the best examples of hooking the interest of children is found in Chapter I of Dr. James Smith's book, *Creative Teaching of Reading and Literature in the Elementary School.*

One day while visiting a classroom, Dr. Smith observed the following teacher comments: "They are such slow learners. I don't believe that any of them have an I.Q. over ninety. And with their poor backgrounds and all added to that, I don't think they are ever going to read."[1] Christmas was two weeks away, and the only evidence of any attention to it was a few purchased cutouts of Santa Claus and a Christmas tree.

Finally Dr. Smith got his chance to work with these children, whom the teacher felt could learn nothing. He brought a tape recorder to class. They had never seen one before. He called it his *magic box.* His first task was to get the children to talk, and he used the tape recorder to get the talk started. He asked the children if he could use his *magic box* to record their voices. He said that sometimes it is hard to remember what to say in a tape recorder so they could say anything that came to mind. The words

---

[1]James Smith, *Creative Teaching of Reading and Literature in the Elementary School* (Boston, Mass.: Allyn and Bacon, Inc., 1966), p. 3.

came fast and furious. Then he said, "I think we'll have some fun together this afternoon with many kinds of magic."[2]

He made a heading on the chalkboard, Words We Want to Know. Of course the first word was magic. He said that before the day was over they were going to make some magic. He drew two large Christmas trees on the chalkboard. He said they were very sad and asked the children if they had any idea why they were so sad. The children replied that the trees needed some decorations. He then placed the word decoration just below magic on the board. He passed out a box of chalk and asked the children to make some decorations.

While some children were making decorations on the chalkboard, he asked others to write a group story about the tree. The name of it was "The Sad Christmas Tree."

> Once there was a Christmas tree.
> It was sad.
> We decorated it.
> Charlie drew stars.
> Melba drew candy canes.
> Kevin drew candles.
> Daniel drew tinsel.
> Maria and Jimmy put presents at the bottom.
> Thomas drew snowflakes.
> Peggy and Walter drew Christmas balls.
> Owen and Willard drew beads.
> Jonah drew wreaths.
> Arthur drew holly.
> Nancy and Sarah drew lights.
> Peter drew a Santa Claus.
> June put a star on top.
> Ellen wrote "Merry Christmas" over it.
> Harry drew a manger.[3]

Before long the trees were decorated with wonderful, childish and creative decorations and the story had been finished. They put the story on tape in the *magic box.* Dr. Smith then said, "They are really nice trees, but they are not like the ones I see when I walk along Genessee Street. How are they different?"[4] In unison the

---

[2] Smith, *Creative Teaching of Reading and Literature,* p. 6.

[3] Smith, *Creative Teaching of Reading and Literature,* p. 8.

[4] Smith, *Creative Teaching of Reading and Literature,* p. 9.

children replied, "They need color." Dr. Smith asked a child to pull down all of the shades and another to stand by the light switch. In the meantime he slid a black light under the tree. The children did not know he had given them florescent chalk. He asked the child at the lights to flip the switch when he said the word *magic.* When all the shades were down, Dr. Smith said, "Let there be magic." The lights went off and the Christmas trees burst into color. Needless to say, the children became very excited. Then they wrote a story about the Magic Christmas Tree. The children were shocked when they suddenly realized that they were learning bigger words than they had ever studied before. They read their stories over and over . . . and they played them back on the *magic box.* Suddenly they realized that two hours had elapsed. As Dr. Smith turned to leave the room, Kevin, the boy whom the teacher felt was hopeless and would never learn to read, asked him if he could read for him.

Dr. Smith, in his explanation of what happens during these experiences says, "So this is what creative teaching does; it catches the magic within children which makes them learn, and it brings it out into the open where you can get at it and work with it."[5]

Effective Activities for Children

How do you catch the magic within each child? You do it by creatively using the myriad of packages that are available today. But· that is not enough; you need more. You need a constant supply of creative ideas that can catch the magic within the child.

The pages that follow are an attempt to whet the appetite on creative activities for children. They are presented with the hope they will stimulate the reader to search for more and better ideas to catch that magic.

Key Words

One of the best ways to develop vocabulary with young children is to develop Key Words. This is a technique developed by Sylvia Ashton-Warner and is reported in her book, *Teacher.* The main reason for using it is the large discrepancy between a child's

---

[5]Smith, *Creative Teaching of Reading and Literature,* p. 11.

speaking vocabulary and the rate at which he is taught new words in beginning reading. To overcome this deficiency, ask the child to give you his word. You write it on a piece of tagboard. Each day he gives you a new word. As his list begins to increase both in difficulty and number, you can begin to do many things with the Key Words. It also becomes readily noticeable that the words the child gives you and the ones presented in the basal text have almost no similarity.

In their book, *Key Words to Reading, A Language Experience Approach Begins,* Barnette, Blakey, Elliott, Sawicki, and Veatch have developed guidelines for the use of Key Words. They are as follows:

A. The word a child gives you must have an emotional impact for him, otherwise it will probably not be retained. You tell the class that you want them to tell you their "best" word, one that makes them feel happy, sad, or angry, or a word that is funny or scary.

B. Have each child whisper his word into your ear. This is a technique that adds intrigue to the activity for some children, while for shy children it is a security factor. In time most children will naturally discard the "whisper technique."

C. Write the word on a 3 x 11 inch card with a felt pen. Let the children name the letters they know and tell them the ones they don't know. Thus, the beginning of letter identification. Point to the wall alphabet if desirable.

D. Have the child trace the word with his finger. Check for left to right, top to bottom direction on the child's writing. Immediately correct any handwriting errors or reversals. It also affords the child an opportunity to "feel" his word as well as name the letters.

E. The child "does something" with his word. The activity is of his own choosing and may be such things as painting a picture of the word, writing "other words" about his word, etc.

F. The next day, the words are reviewed. *The words the child does not know are discarded.* Words the child does not remember are not significant to him. No attempt should be made to teach the word. Throw away such comments as "You will get a good one next time."[6]

[6]Eleanor Barnette, Janis Blakey, Geraldine Elliot, Florence Sawicki, and Jeanette Veatch, *Key Words to Reading: A Language Experience Approach Begins* (Published by the Authors, Tempe, Arizona, July, 1969, out of print, out of stock, Revised Edition, C.E. Merrill, 1973), pp. 25-26.

Ideas for Using Key Words

1. Ask the child to classify the words according to your directions. (Toys, beginning sound of____, endings, etc.)
2. Arrange the words alphabetically.
3. Use the words for a story.
4. Paint a picture of the word.
5. Exchange your words with a partner to see if you know each other's words.
6. Select one word and build a story around it.
7. Play some reading games using your words.
8. Read one of your words to a partner and see if he can find a word in his pack that begins the same as your word.
9. Together with a partner, see how many of your words are related. (Example: ball-bounce, spoon-eat)
10. Make a dictionary with your words.
11. Group leader says: "Show me a _____ food, part of the body, name of someone, an animal, a plant, a sound, member of your family, shape, etc."

Effective Ideas for Reading

Idea #1

Decorate several boxes and place letters of the alphabet on each of them. Begin with the consonant sounds. Obtain objects with the same beginning sound as the box. Ask the children to say the word as they drop it in the correct box.

Idea #2

Make a large drawing of an animal, clown, or something that is motivating to the children. Print letters of the alphabet on various parts of the drawing. Ask the children to throw beanbags on the letters. They must name the letter they hit.

Idea #3

Make letters out of paper, pipe cleaners, or any other material that is available. Ask the children to display them in order. You could also use them for making words, separating vowels from consonants, or for kinesthetic practice.

Idea #4

The names of colors can be learned by matching the word with the color. On one side of a tag sheet place several colors. On the other side paste a picture showing the color. Attach string near the word. When the strings are tied to the picture the task is complete.

Idea #5

Put a consonant on the chalkboard. Give the two groups catalogs and give them five minutes to find as many words as they can that have the same beginning sound. This could be done with endings, vowel combinations, blends, or numerous other things.

Idea #6

Put a number of small objects in a box. Make sure the objects represent things that are familiar to the child. Ask him to pick one out and name it. Upon naming it he should give another word that begins the same. Each correct response is a point. After the lesson is over the teacher can teach a lesson in classification by grouping the objects around a variety of things.

Idea #7

Cut a circle out of poster board and paste on it several pictures, each with a different beginning sound, ending, vowel sounds, etc. Make a spinner out of a brad and a paper clip and put it in the center. Then make up a series of pictures, many with the same beginning sounds, and paste them on the tag. The children spin and say the name the spinner points to. Then they select a picture which begins with the same sound.

Idea #8

Make a pocket chart with several rows of openings. Near the left side of the chart place several pictures, each with different beginning sounds. Give the child a number of pictures and have them put them in the correct slot.

Idea #9

Two circles, one smaller than the other, are fastened together through their centers in order to rotate freely. The centers may be fastened by a large brass fastener. Initial consonants are printed on the large circle so that different words can be formed. By rotating the larger circle initial consonants can be combined with the same phonogram. This device can be used to stress initial sounds, common phonograms, final sounds, etc.

Idea #10

A line of cars, snowcats, motorcycles or bicycles is drawn on a sheet of tagboard. Each vehicle has a slit with a pocket pasted behind it. A word is printed on each vehicle. Rhyming words are placed in an envelope on the back of the caravan. The child is to sort out the words and place them in the correct vehicle.

Idea #11

Ten or more sections are marked off on a path. Two players each take a space capsule and set of cards rhyming with those on the path. The first player reads his first word aloud. If it rhymes with the first word on the path, he moves his capsule to the first place. If it is not the same, he may not move. He places the card at the bottom of the pack and the next player takes a turn.

Idea #12

A card is divided into squares with a picture pasted on each box. Words that rhyme with the picture are placed in an envelope attached to the card. The child is to place the words on the correct picture.

Idea #13

Using flannel or oaktag, cut out a clown into pieces like a puzzle. On each piece of puzzle write a word beginning with a consonant blend. Place the clown on the flannel board. A child selects a part of the clown. If the child can supply a word that begins like the one on the section of the clown, he may remove that section and help make the clown disappear.

Idea #14

Slits are cut into the tail of a tagboard fish so a card can slide up and down in the opening. Part of the word is printed on the fish, and the final consonant on the card. The child slides the card to form new words by changing the final consonant.

Idea #15

The bottom of a box is divided like a puzzle. Each section has a word on it. The same puzzle is re-cut using words that have the same final consonants as those in the box. The child matches the words that end the same. This game is self-checking.

Idea #16

Sentences are printed on a card which is then cut in half like a puzzle. Several of these are placed in an envelope. They are put together and read.

Idea #17

An oaktag circle is cut and an arrow is fastened to it by means of a brad. Numerals are written around the edge of the circle. A child spins the arrow on the disc. Questions corresponding to each numeral are written on a card attached to the back of the circle. The child answers the questions that correspond to the numeral the arrow is pointing to.

Idea #18

Select a rectangular piece of poster paper. Make a two-inch margin all the way around and divide it up into spaces. Write vocabulary words in the spaces. Some spaces may be used as penalties or rewards. Each player throws the dice and moves clockwise the number of spaces indicated, beginning with home. He must read the word he lands on. If he cannot, he goes back to where he was until his next turn.

Idea #19

Cut up many one-inch squares. Write one letter of the alphabet on each square. There should be four complete sets of the alphabet. Put these cards into a small box. To play, the children lay all the cards face down in the center of the table. Each player draws four cards. He will try to use all or part of his cards to spell a word.

When one child spells a word, he wins a point and the game begins. If no one can spell a word, each child takes another card.

Idea #20

On strips of paper write compound words. Cut the words in half and place them in a box. The children try to put the words together again.

Idea #21

The second child guesses the word the first child has read silently from a pack of cards. The first child gives clues to the word.

Idea #22

One-inch squares are cut out of wood. Each side has a letter printed on it. Words are made with the blocks.

Idea #23

A part of a word is written on a clothespin. The other part is on a card. When the two match, pin them together.

Idea #24

Write a story on a chart. Leave every sixth word blank. The child is asked to fit in words from a pack of cards to complete the story. If necessary, put the first letter of each word in the blank.

Idea #25

One child flashes a word card. The child in the game who can match the flashed card from his hand does so. He then becomes the flasher.

Idea #26

Deal four or more cards to each child in the game. The first child reads a word. All the others who have cards with that vowel sound give this card to the first child. The game ends when one child runs out of cards.

Idea #27

Take several shoe boxes and mark them consonants, endings, long vowels, short vowels, blends, etc. Give the children a set of word cards. They are to place them in the correct box.

Idea #28

Three cards are dealt out on which are printed syllables. Each player draws and discards until he can make a three syllable word.

Idea #29

Make an obstacle course on a piece of tagboard. On the course have rewards as well as penalties. One child throws the dice. He moves the number of times indicated by the dice. If he lands on certain spaces, he is required to choose a card. The cards are made of multi-syllable words. He can move as many spaces as there are syllables in the word providing he knows how many syllables there are. If he is caught moving the incorrect number of spaces, his partner can ask him to begin over.

Idea #30

There are two decks of cards, one of root words and one of suffixes. The child draws a card from each pile. If he can make a word he gets to keep it. If he cannot, he places the cards back in the pile. The winner is the child having the most pairs.

Idea #31

Write sentences from new vocabulary words on colored strips of construction paper. Cut the sentences up. Exchange the sentences with a story partner. See if the story partner can arrange the words into the sentences as they were first written.

Idea #32

Make duplicate sets of word cards on oaktag. Deal the cards one at a time until each player has five cards. The remainder of the pack is placed in the center of the table face down. The object of the game is to get as many pairs of cards as possible. The player on the dealer's left starts by asking any child he wishes for a card that matches one of the cards which he holds in his hand. For example: he may hold the card "ghost" and he asks someone for that card. If the child asked has the word, he must give it to him. This player continues to ask for another card until he is unsuccessful. When the one asked does not have the card he says, "Go to the woodpile." The child then draws from the pack and the next player takes a turn.

Idea #33

Make cards of oaktag with the following words on them:

hat	shell	will	all	sing	sand	look
cat	well	spill	tall	bing	band	book
rat	fell	fill	wall	wing	land	brook
sat	tell	bill	ball	bring	hand	shook

Next make four cards having the words *change over* on them. Deal out five cards. The child to the left of the dealer plays any card, naming it. The next player either plays a card that rhymes or begins with the same letter. For example: If *bill* has been played, *fill* rhyming with bill or *band* beginning with the same letter could be played. If a child cannot play, he draws from the extra cards until he can play or has drawn three cards. If he has the card "change over" he may play that card and name a word that can be played upon. The first person out of cards wins the game.

Idea #34

Print single phrases or words on slips of paper. Write a numerical value from 1-5 for each in the upper right hand corner of each slip. The slips are placed face down on the table. The players take turns selecting a slip and reading it. If the player can read the slip correctly, he keeps it. If he doesn't read it correctly, the player replaces the slip and the next player takes his turn. The winner is the player with the highest score.

Idea #35

Make forty cards, each containing a one syllable word. There must be at least two cards with the same vowel sound. Deal four cards to each player and place the rest face down in a pile in the middle of the table. The first player reads clearly any of his cards aloud. Any player who has a card with the same vowel sound pronounces his word and the first player must give him his card. The second player then lays these two cards in front of him. The first player draws a card from the pile to replace the card he has lost. The next player draws a card from the pile to replace the card he has lost. The next player calls his card. If no one has a card with the same vowel sound, the next player calls a card. The player with the most cards in front of him is the winner.

Idea #36

Divide the group into two teams. Write a command on the board and erase it, or write a command on a card and show it before the children's eyes for a moment. Call on someone to perform the command. Members of each group are given a turn. If the command is carried out by the one the leader called upon, his group scores.

Idea #37

The leader puts a long list of words on the board. The leader chooses a word and says: "I am thinking of a word that_____." This is a good game because the leader can use every reading skill he wishes. Examples would be: a word that begins like_____, a word that has the blend_____, vowels or vowel combinations, endings, prefixes, suffixes, a word that rhymes with_____, a word that is a synonym to_____, etc.

Idea #38

Write an adjective on each of many word cards. Line them up on the chalkboard. Then write a noun or something that can be described by the words on the board. When the child has finished selecting the descriptive words, have him read them to you or members of the group to see if they agree.

Idea #39

The teacher prepares cards in sets of four, printing on each card a noun belonging to a certain group or class. Line the children up and give out one card of each set. When each child has a card, the teacher shuffles the rest of the cards and flashes them one at a time before the group. The pupil holding a card belonging to the same set as the one the teacher flashes says *stop!* and is given the teacher's card. Each child must say the word and give the reason as to why it should belong to him. If no one responds, they hold their cards up and the teacher checks them. The child holding the card is told why it should belong to him. Then the teacher places this card back in the pack to be flashed again later on. Four cards make a book. When a child has a book, he is given another card. The person with the most books wins. This can be done with endings, beginnings, vowel combinations, etc.

Idea #40

Make scrabbled words on cards. See how fast the students can make words out of them.

Idea #41

As new words are learned, they are placed on cards. Later, small numbers can be placed in the corner of the card. Make a large wheel out of cardboard. Let the children spin the dial. The number the dial stops on is the word he must read. Have several words with the same number. If he gets the word or words right, he scores the number of points on the card in the lower right hand corner. As the words get harder, they are given more points. The highest number of points that can be gotten is four. The highest point total wins.

Idea #42

Make ten one, two and three syllable words on cards. Ask the children to sort them out. The first one to get them all correct is the winner.

Idea #43

Pin words on a dart board. The child throws the darts at the board. If he hits a word he can keep it providing he can pronounce it. Each child has three darts. Each word card has a different number in the lower right hand corner. After all three darts are thrown, he counts up the point total of all darts that hit the word cards and are pronounced correctly.

Idea #44

Make a deck of cards of verbs. Each player must give at least one adverb. The adverb has to be different for each player for the same word.

Idea #45

A number of large cards with small pictures of various objects pasted on them will be needed. Have an envelope attached to the cards with a series of words on them. The children are told to place the various word cards on the correct pictures on the chart.

Idea #46

Make several sets of long and short vowel signs for each vowel (Ā Ē Ī Ō Ū and Ă Ĕ Ĭ Ŏ Ŭ). Make a deck of words using each vowel sound. Shuffle the cards. Give each player a set of cards. At a given signal each student tries to get as many words under the right vowel sound as he can.

Idea #47

A picture representing a stream is drawn on the board or is made of heavy paper. Many stones are located in the stream. Upon each stone is a word. If the child can name and use in a sentence each word, he crosses the stream. If not, the child slips and falls in the stream. Hopscotch is a variation of this game. Place cards in the formation of hopscotch. Each player takes a turn trying to hop through by saying the words correctly. When a word is missed the player hops back out by saying the words and it is the next player's turn.

Idea #48

Play bingo with words. The leader calls out a word. If found on your card, place a bean seed over it. The winner is the same as in bingo.

Idea #49

Paste several pictures on a piece of oaktag. Prepare an envelope containing small squares. In the middle of the square type the initial letters of the name of the objects in the picture. Lower case letters are used. A dot or mark at the bottom of the letter will prevent inversions. The child places the letter on the pictures.

Idea #50

Children sort out word cards and put them into boxes that are marked short or long vowels, blends, etc. The player with the most correct responses is the winner.

Idea #51

Give each child a piece of paper that has been marked off into nine squares. Put about eleven or twelve of the new vocabulary words on the chalkboard. Have each child put any nine of these words on his squares in any order he chooses. A caller pronounces the words in random order. Each player covers three words in a row in any direction, raises his hand, pronounces the three words as a check, and wins the game.

Idea #52

The children sit on the floor in a circle. Cards are placed face down on the floor in the center of the circle. Each child has a turn. He takes a card from the pack. If he knows it, he may say it and keep it. If not, he will put it face up on the floor. The next child may take that card if he wants to, or another card from the pack.

Idea #53

The teacher holds up a large picture. The children are to find a picture of theirs that begins with the same sound.

Idea #54

The children sit in a circle with one child seated in the middle with a ball. He rolls the ball to any one child, says a word, and that child must give a word that rhymes. If he is correct, he gets to sit in the middle of the circle with the ball. If not, the child in the center tries another person.

Idea #55

The teacher makes twenty-four small cards. On each of these cards, place pairs of words that are sometimes confused. The cards are distributed; each player receives one card. The first player lays down his card in front of him and reads the two words. He then must give one sentence in which the two words are used. If he does this, he keeps the card in front of him. If he cannot do this, he puts the card at the bottom of the pile, and the second player has a chance to give his sentence orally. Cards are drawn from the pile as the game progresses. The game continues until all the cards are on the table. The player with the most cards is the winner.

Idea #56

The leader begins this game by saying, "I am thinking of a word which means about the same as *unhappy.*" The other players guess in turn by saying, for example, "Is the word sorrowful?" Whoever guesses the word is the leader.

Idea #57

On a chart, place a series of pictures with common nouns and leave space for children to add other names for the same things as they find them in their reading.

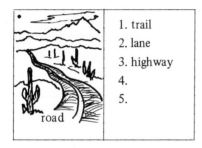

	1. trail
	2. lane
	3. highway
	4.
road	5.

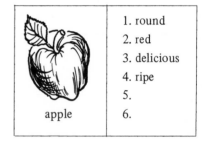

	1. round
	2. red
	3. delicious
	4. ripe
	5.
apple	6.

Idea #58

Make a large wheel from tagboard with prefixes or suffixes around the rim. As each player spins the wheel, he must give a word that ends with the suffix or begins with the prefix at which the spinner stops.

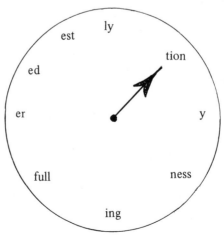

Idea #59

Draw a tic-tac-toe diagram. ⊞ Instead of using *Xs* and *Os,* one person could use the nouns, his partner the verbs, or one person could be proper nouns and his partner common nouns. The first person to get a consecutive row across, down, or diagonally of nouns or verbs is the winner. Add a third horizontal line and a third vertical line to make the game more interesting.

Idea #60

Write the name of a famous person vertically. The student makes a root word with each letter. Add a prefix or suffix to it to make another word.

Book Sharing

Increasingly, there is a concern on the part of some perceptive educators about what reading instruction is ultimately to accomplish. For the past many years there has been a great preoccupation on the part of the reading establishment with *how to read.* Today that emphasis is shifting to a balanced one of *how to* and *lifetime commitment.*

One program that has that balance is called personalized or individualized reading. This program is built upon the theory that children should be able to seek their own books, self-select their own books, and read them at their own pace.[7] It further says that they should spend a great deal of their time conferencing with their teachers on a one-to-one basis and then grouped for skills around common needs.

An important part of personalized or individualized reading is book sharing. Book sharing is that part of the program that helps children excite other children about reading through the use of creative activities. Some of the techniques that have been found helpful are listed below. They should be of great help to auxiliaries as they try to interest children in reading.

Book Sharing Ideas

Prepare a filmstrip to be shown by winding from one cardboard

---

[7] Walter Barbe, *Educator's Guide to Personalized Reading Instruction* (Englewood Cliffs, N.J.: Prentice-Hall, Inc., 1961), p. 3.

cylinder to another. These cylinders can be slipped on dowel rods attached to a base or made with a cardboard box.

Prepare a story dramatization to present to another group. Hold a panel discussion with several students who have read the book. Part could talk for the book and part against the book.

Make: a mural, a rebus, a diorama, a collage, an alliteration, or a mobile.

Write a letter to a friend telling him about your book.

Make radio announcements to advertise a book. (newspaper, TV)

Make puppets to depict a story that has been read.

The teacher reads a book and shares it with the students.

Write a new ending for the book.

Make a book jacket for the book.

Make a table of contents for the book if it doesn't have one.

Make a time line of events in the story.

Write a movie script for the book.

Draw a picture depicting a favorite character of the book.

Write a poem about the book.

Give a summary of the book, telling what you liked and what you didn't like.

Make a scrapbook by information suggested in the book.

Make lists of facts that you have learned.

Dress like one of the characters in the book.

Fold a piece of paper two times so there are four squares.

Draw four pictures that best represent the book.

Use the P.A. system to tell the children about the book.

Write a letter to the librarian to be put in the library.

Make a model out of wood, clay, etc. of the book.

Write a letter to the author.

Give a talk about how the author used interesting words.

Pantomime an interesting part of the book.

Draw a comic strip of the book.

Compare two books written by the same author.

Select a book of the week, book of the semester, book of the year.

Oral Reading

If the professional staff doesn't provide the auxiliary staff with a constant flow of creative ideas, there is a danger that reading could degenerate into a "You read to me and I will read to you" process. Oral reading, one of the most important tools in all of reading instruction, is oftentimes the most misused. Dr. George Spache, in his book, *Reading in the Elementary School,* has this to say about oral reading:

> Oral reading, in the basal reader program, has developed a number of most undesirable aspects which are supported and abetted by the very nature of the basal series. We know of no manual for a basal series which suggests these practices but believe they are a logical outcome of the overemphasis upon the importance of the basic vocabulary. One of these faulty practices is the roundrobin or circle reading seen in most of today's classrooms. A reading group assembles in a semicircle around the teacher and the children take turns reading aloud to the group. All the children use the same book and attempt to follow silently as each pupil has his oral reading turn. About the only real purpose for this practice is to permit the teacher to observe the accuracy with which each pupil reads the words of the text. At worst, this practice violates the known fact that both oral reading and comprehension are superior when silent reading of a selection precedes oral. The relevant research indicates that this circle reading is probably one of the most effective devices yet discovered for practicing poor reading. What literally happens in this almost universal technique is that the listeners are forced to attempt to follow and imitate the halting reading of the leader. As a result, as Gilbert has shown, the children's reading performances are worse when reading in the circle than they would normally be.[8]

Because the auxiliary will use this technique often in his work with elementary age children, the following suggestions are given as appropriate ways to use oral reading:

A. Choral reading
B. Verification of facts (Find the paragraph that says . . .)
C. Reading original stories or poems
D. Vocabulary review (Can you find the new word?)
E. Read orally to give an interpretation of a selection
F. Oral expression (Do you think Mary liked to . . .)
G. Reading a character part

---

[8]*Reading in the Elementary School* (Boston, Mass.: Allyn and Bacon, Inc., 1964), p. 85.

H. Dramatization
I. Reading news reports or announcements
J. Encouraging specific kinds of expression
K. Reading orally to support the position taken in a discussion
L. Read orally for enjoyment
M. Reading a script for a radio or T.V. program
N. To develop eye-voice span
O. Read directions for making something
P. Read literary passages
Q. Reading jokes or riddles
R. Read a story while someone pantomimes it
S. Make a tape recording of oral reading
T. Practice enunciation and phrasing
U. Reading to visitors to the classroom or group

Effective Ideas for Spelling

Idea #1

Duplicate a list of simple sentences or write them on the chalkboard. Each sentence demonstrates the correct usage of a word from the class, the spelling list, or a child's language experience list, but the word is missing from the sentence. Children fill in the missing word. For example: The best place to find the definition of a word is in the _____. Sometimes they may need a hint. In that case give them the first letter or letter sound.

Idea #2

Place a word on the chalkboard in column form, then print the word backwards in column form next to it. The player must make words that begin and end with the letters that are opposite each other, or that have that letter combination. For example:

On the chalkboard		*Children in Group*	
T	K	T ac	K
A	S	A	S tronaut
S	A	S	A ber
K	T	K i	T e

Idea #3

This spelling game can be played with two persons or with small groups. Draw two gallows on the chalkboard. Under each gallow draw the number of blank spaces for a spelling word. The other person or team must fill in the blanks by guessing until they know what the word is. As the name of the person is called upon, he guesses a letter that may fit. If the letter is correct it is put in its proper place on the board. If the same letter appears twice in a word it is put in both places. If the letter named is not in the word, then a head or a part of the body is drawn in a noose on the gallows. With each word missed, additional parts of the body are added to the man on the gallows until he is officially hung. The first team to get its man hung is the loser. (Establish ahead of time how many parts the man will have.)

Idea #4

Draw the trunk and main limbs of a tree on the board and label each limb with a phonetic sound. Each child has a turn to name a word that contains the sound and to spell the word. If a player is successful, he is allowed to draw and color a leaf on that limb of the tree. Bonus words can be added as oranges or other fruit hanging on the tree.

Idea #5

Make a word tree for your group. Ask the children to put a new word on each of the leaves. When the tree is full, ask them to repeat the words. Rewards can be given for each word pronounced correctly. If playing the game in teams, the person pronouncing the most words is the winner.

Idea #6

A word from the child's spelling list is announced by the leader. Each student tries to find the word in his dictionary. The first to find it is the winner. He tells the page number and the definition in his own words. He must give the definition to the satisfaction of the leader.

Idea #7

Cut one-inch squares from oaktag or filing cards. Place a letter on each square, making extras of vowels and double consonants. Each child has his own set of squares. The teacher calls out a word and the children spell the word at their tables using the squares. The first child to finish receives a point. Extra points can be given for making more than one word.

Idea #8

Make several three or four word crossword puzzles for the children to solve. Make certain the words spell vertically and horizontally.

Idea #9

List several words in one column on the chalkboard and list the first and last letter of a synonym for each word in the second column, such as: aid—h— —p. Set a time limit for filling in the blanks. This can also be done with antonyms and homonyms.

Idea #10

Write each letter of the alphabet on a piece of tagboard. If large groups are used, do it several times. Place all the letters in a box. From this box have each pupil draw out seven letters without looking at them. Each pupil should use as many of his letters as he can to make a word. Then have each pupil tell the group the letters he drew and the word he made.

Idea #11

Select a series of words to which letters can be added to make new words. Give a clue along with a definition for the group to complete each one. For example: Add letters to SUN to make a day of the week, or add a letter to EAR to show the making of money. This game can also be played with prefixes and suffixes.

Idea #12

Write several words on the board from the children's spelling list and ask them to make as many sentences as they can using the words. This game could be extended to definitions or making a story out of the sentences.

Idea #13

Gain speed in spelling and practice in listening by spelling the words out instead of saying the words. Instead of saying "We went to town," they would say, "We went to T-O-W-N."

Idea #14

Draw two blocks, each containing sixteen squares. The first child from each team writes a letter in one square in the top row. A child from the other team then adds a letter and so on, alternating teams seeing who can spread a word the furthest. Ask the children about what kinds of letters they have discovered are easiest to make words. Ask them why. The game can be made more interesting by making larger squares with more blocks.

Idea #15

Put a list of words on the board with their letters scrambled. The pupils must unscramble the words orally, at the board or on paper.

Idea #16

Using the spelling list, find as many of the words as you can in a newspaper article.

Idea #17

Take a word from the list and *act it out*. Set a time limit of thirty seconds. The pupil who guesses the word presents his word to the group.

Idea #18

Each corner of the room is a base for your baseball diamond. Divide the group into two teams and select two good spellers to act as the pitcher for each team to *toss* the words to the other team. Write out two lists of words of equal difficulty for the pitchers to use or let the teams select words to use for their pitcher. Each player at bat is given a word. If it is spelled correctly he gets a single and moves one base ahead. If the word is missed he is given an out. Each team is allowed three *outs* before the other team takes the field. As each batter wins his *single* other members move forward. *Home runs* are recorded as a player moves around all bases. The pitcher can decide if a word is worth a single, double, triple or home run.

Idea #19

Take a very colorful paragraph from a book. Replace some of the descriptive words with ordinary words and underline them. Have the pupils substitute these words with more effective words.

Idea #20

A word is given to a group. The object of the game is to select a synonym for that word. Each player who makes a correct response gets a point. Do the same for antonyms and homonyms.

Idea #21

Write a series of long words on the chalkboard. Ask the pupils to make as many words as they can from these words. An example could be: accountability: tab, count, ability, account. Use words that have several vowels.

Idea #22

Give the children cutouts of fish. Ask them to write their favorite new words on the cutout and put a paper clip on the fish. Place fish in a bowl and make a fishing line out of string. At the end of the string attach a magnet. The child picks out a word and tries to spell it. If he spells it correctly, he can keep it. If not, he puts it back in the box.

Idea #23

Using the newspaper or news stories on television, make a list of words that are prominent in the news. Discuss the words and use them for spelling games. Emphasize meaning, usage and etymology of the word.

Idea #24

Discuss the meaning of *categories*. When the pupils have paper and pencils ready, announce a specific category. Examples could be animals, space, states, words with prefixes, root word port, etc. See how many words they can write under each category.

Idea #25

The first player on one team spells a word. Then the first player of the second team spells a word beginning with the last letter of that word. The second team player must then spell a "chain word."

Idea #26

Have each pupil write ANTHROPOLOGY vertically on a sheet of paper. At a given signal, they should write as many words as they can that relate to that word. Other words such as history, geography, technology, etc. could be used also.

Idea #27

Ask the children to:

Read a story and find action words for a spelling test.
Read a story and find the nouns for a spelling test.
Make a list of rhyming words.
Make a list of words with the same vowel sound.
Make a list of sounds you hear in nature.
Make a list of tastes.
Make a list of sounds like rain.
Make a list of smells.

Idea #28

Each child in the group should have his own box with alphabetized dividers. Words are selected both by the teacher and through the child's own language. About five words per day is all that should be presented if this is used with children who have difficulty in spelling. The teacher writes a word on a 3 x 6 card and asks the child to pronounce it. The child spells it for the teacher. The child is given a card and writes the word four times kinesthetically with his finger. The child then turns the card over and writes the word with his pencil. The teacher checks the word and the child files it. Review the words at the end of the period. At the end of the week select five of the words for a spelling test. These words can be used for stories, study of prefixes, suffixes, root words and many other kinds of phonetic analysis.

Effective Writing Ideas

Idea #1

Mount pictures on manila folders. On the inside of the folders facing the picture, print words that can be used to make a story about the picture.

Idea #2

Imagine what it is like to walk on the moon. Write a story about it and send it to an astronaut. Ask him if your perception is correct.

Idea #3

To improve sentences have children write a basic sentence on a colored strip of paper. Cut the sentence up so that each word is separate. Place them in an envelope and exchange. The partner assembles the jumbled words and improves the sentence with another colored strip of paper. Write only the words needed for improvement. This, too, is cut up and placed in the proper part of the sentence. He then shows his partner how he improved his sentence.

Idea #4

Write letters to parents, ill classmates, grandparents, etc., telling them about the activities in school.

Idea #5

Write a story that ends like this:

- A. Then I woke up.
- B. He will never be forgotten.
- C. Everyone can come out now.
- D. This made John the happiest boy in town.
- E. Some guys have all the luck.
- F. I'll never do that again.
- G. I am glad you won this time.
- H. They have been the best of friends ever since.

Idea #6

A pun is the humorous use of a word in a way that suggests two meanings. Write as many as you can. Some examples are: "You hit the nail on the head." "I'll see if I can dig something up for you, said the gravedigger."

Idea #7

Have each child bring a box with an object in it. Regulate the size of the box and the kind of object. Exchange boxes. Write a series of questions to ask the owner. See if your questions will reveal the identity of the object in the box.

Idea #8

Write a cinquain. The pattern for a cinquain is as follows:

First line—one word—giving title
Second line—two words—describing title
Third line—three words—expressing action
Fourth line—four words—expressing a feeling
Fifth line—one word—a synonym for the title

Idea #9

Write a limerick using words from your spelling list. The pattern for a limerick is A-A-B-B-A. (The first and second lines rhyme—lines three and four rhyme—and line five rhymes with lines one and two.)

Idea #10

Write a couplet poem. An example would be:

Black cat,
Sat, sat,
On mat,
Poor cat!

Idea #11

Listen to an unfinished tape recorded story and make up an ending.

Idea #12

Provide a picture for each student or have each student bring his own. Write a creative story from the picture. Exchange stories and read.

Idea #13

Have the whole group make a language experience story. Then ask each child in the group to make up his own ending.

Idea #14

Ask the children to finish these sentences:

    I would like to see_____
    I would like to hear_____
    I would like to feel_____
    I would like to smell_____
    I would like to go_____

Idea #15

Write a language experience story by writing a beginning sentence on the chalkboard. The class chooses among the sentences suggested by class members and the story is completed. The story can be read back, analyzed for structure, or cut up and put back together.

Idea #16

Have all of the children close their eyes. Pass out an object for all of them to feel. After a short time ask all of them to write about it.

Idea #17

Write a story about a dream you have had.

Idea #18

Clip a bunch of headlines from newspapers. Ask the children to draw one out and write about it.

Idea #19

Make one envelope for each of the five parts of the story:

A. main character   D. the problem
B. character trait   E. what happens
C. scene or setting

Have the pupils suggest what will be written on the slips to go into each envelope. The slips in the first envelope will have on them suggestions for the main character in the story the children will write. The slips in the second envelope will have suggestions for the character trait of the main character. For example, the child may draw from the first envelope a slip with a *child of eight* printed on it: this would be the main character for his story. A slip would be drawn from each envelope to get the component parts of his story.

Idea #20

Write haiku. Haiku is a kind of Japanese poetry. If often describes one of the seasons of the year or expresses a very special feeling. Haiku has only three lines. The first line has five syllables, the second line has seven syllables, and the third line has five syllables. It does not need to rhyme. The emphasis should be upon one thought expressing a feeling.

Idea #21

Give the children a cartoon or funny strip with the captions cut off. Have them write a conversation or caption which fits the action.

Idea #22

Ask each child to keep a journal. This is a special folder where children can write exactly how they feel. The teacher never looks in the journal unless the child wants to share his writings.

Idea #23

Write a story around one of the following titles:

A. Santa Claus   G. I Couldn't believe My Eyes
B. My Secret   H. Outer Space
C. Apollo to the Moon   I. This Was My Lucky Day
D. I Wonder   J. Was I Embarrassed
E. Night Gallery   K. My First Camping Trip

F. My One Wish   L. How About Me?

M. Who Am I?

Idea #24

Write an autobiography.

Idea #25

Write as many words as you can think of that have recently been added to our language. Write as many words as you can think of that have been dropped because of disuse.

Idea #26

Trace the derivation of a word.

Idea #27

Make a chart for the *word of the week*. Each week add to the list. At the end of a certain period of time, use these words for writing a story.

Idea #28

Use one of the following incomplete sentences to make a story:

If I had a million dollars I_____
One dark night_____
Last night I dreamed_____
I'm not really me, I'm_____
To me school is_____
My parents_____
Love is_____
I feel sad when_____

Idea #29

Write a paragraph to support or contradict a common saying. Some are:

A. Look before you leap.
B. A rolling stone gathers no moss.
C. Still water runs deep.
D. Haste makes waste.
E. The early bird gets the worm.

Idea #30

Interpret the following figurative language:

A. Hit the nail on the head. E. Put your foot down.
B. Ride herd. F. He is a gem.
C. I am all thumbs. G. You are a sparkplug.
D. The windswept prairies. H. Bring home the bacon.
I. Grow like a weed.

Idea #31

Take a sheet of typing paper and tear a design in the middle of it. After you have finished, decide what your design looks like. Then add things like legs, arms, wheels, horns, etc., to make it even more realistic. Write a story about your picture.

Effective Ideas in Mathematics

Idea #1

Choose one child who stands before the group and makes a statement, such as "I am thinking of a number that is one ten and three ones. Those who think they know what the number is, raise your hands." The leader calls on someone to go to the board to write the number, which in this case is thirteen. If what the latter writes is correct, he becomes the leader.

Idea #2

A series of consecutive numbers from one to eight is placed on the legs of an octopus. All but one child hides his eyes while the one child removes a number from one of the legs of the octopus. The child who is chosen to be *it* tries to name the missing number as he looks at the remaining legs of the animal.

Idea #3

Divide the group into two teams. The leader sets a large clock and asks the players to set their clocks the same as the large clock. A variation is to write the time on the board and ask the children to set the clock.

Idea #4

On a tagboard sheet, make a drawing of a stream. On one side of the stream have the players. On the other side is something good, like grandmother's house, candy, etc. Put problems on small sheets of tagboard and place them in the stream. You can cross the' stream by answering all of the problems correctly. If all responses are correct ones, the child chooses another set of problems and another child. If one of the combinations is missed, you fall into the stream and must dry off while another child takes a turn.

Idea #5

Make two sets of number cards with 0 to 9 on them. Give each team a set of cards. The leader calls out a two digit number. The two players who have those numbers must line up to make the number. The team whose members make correct responses first scores a point.

Idea #6

Each pupil is given a number. The teacher says, "I am calling 2 and 4" (or any combination that seems appropriate). The pupil who has the number 6 (if addition) or 2 (if subtraction) answers, "This is 6" or "This is 2."

Idea #7

Draw a circle on the chalkboard. You will need as many circles as there are teams. The circles should have numbers written around the edge only. The number in the center, or the multiplier, is written in later. Numbers are put in different order around the circle. Multipliers may be varied to meet the needs of each child playing the game. A pupil from each team goes to the board and faces the group. The teacher writes in the multipliers. At a given signal, the pupils face the board and write the product beside the outside numbers. After one minute the student stops. The answers are erased after they are corrected and new multipliers are used.

Idea #8

Place ten or more flash cards on the chalkboard. At a given signal, the child is asked to write the answers above the combinations.

Idea #9

Use any of the four basic operations to make up problems. Write the problems in the holes of egg cartons. Put a button in one hole. Close the container and shake. Open the carton and give the answer to the problem with the button on it. Look on the back to see if you are correct.

Idea #10

Take any number, reverse it, then subtract it. The remainder will always be divisible by what number?

Idea #11

Take any two numbers and place one alongside the other. Then take two more and put directly under them. Add the column both ways. What have you discovered? Example:

$$6 \text{ plus } 8 \underline{\hspace{1cm}}$$
$$3 \text{ plus } 9 \underline{\hspace{1cm}}$$
$$\underline{\hspace{1cm}} \ \underline{\hspace{1cm}} \ \boxed{}$$

Idea #12

Two concentric circles are drawn on the chalkboard about one foot apart, with the diameter of the inner circle about one foot in length, making the diameter of the outer circle three feet. Number combinations are written around the track. The first player shakes a die and moves the number indicated. He then solves the problem. If correct, he stays where he is. If not, he must start over.

Idea #13

Provide an empty box for each child in the group and about twenty small objects. Ask them to solve certain equations by using the objects. (15 plus 8 minus 6 plus 2 equals . . .)

Idea #14

Each row of children is a separate team. Assign a multiplication combination to each row. Each child multiplies the answer of the child in front of him by the multiplier in the combination assigned to his row. To give each child practice with both large and small combinations, start the paper at the back of the row every other time. The teacher checks each team's work before declaring the winner. Each row could be assigned the same multiplication combination, and the first row to finish with all correct is the winner.

Idea #15

You will need two teams of five to nine players each. A baseball diamond is drawn on the chalkboard. You then need two or more numbers from 1 through 5 written at each base and a number between 6 and 10 in the pitcher's box. The teacher points to the number in the pitcher's box and to one of the numbers at first base. The player at bat must give the difference between those two numbers. The same is done at each of the other bases. If a player does not miss any of the answers, he scores. If he misses any of them he is out. After three outs, the sides change.

Idea #16

Find one number that will fit in the corner of the puzzle so that each side will add up to a total of 21. Use the same number in all four corners.

X	5	4	X
8	X	X	2
1	X	X	7
X	9	0	X

Idea #17

Add the numbers in the first horizontal row. Supply each of the missing numbers in the other rows so that each row will have an equal sum. Add the numbers in the vertical row. Add the numbers so that each row will also have sums that are equal.

8	15	1
2		13
11	3	
14		4
5		

Idea #18

Take two pieces of tagboard (5 x 12) and fasten them together with both ends open. Make a slide slightly smaller with number combinations on it. Put the answers for each combination directly behind them. Cut a window on the front and back so you can self-check as soon as you solve the problem.

Idea #19

Make a ditto with a small circle in the middle. Put a fraction in this space. On the outside of the circle place several other fractions. The child closes his eyes and puts his pencil on the paper. He then adds, subtracts, multiplies or divides this fraction with the one in the circle.

Idea #20

Make a chart with 36 squares. One square is the starting place and arrows are drawn through each square, with *HOME* as the finishing spot. Put a numeral in each square. Make up a packet of cards. The child chooses a card and divides that number by the first one on the chart. He may move as many places as there is a remainder.

Idea #21

On four pieces of tagboard write Whole Numbers, Mixed Numbers, Improper Fractions, and Proper Fractions. Then make ten cards for each of them. (Example: 6, 1½, 9/7, ¼). The child is to see how fast he can put the cards under the proper heading.

Idea #22

Make a ditto with many numerals on it. On some of them place a line ahead of the numeral, and on the rest place a line behind the numeral. The child is asked to write the numeral that comes before and after the one on the page. The first to complete the page is the winner.

Idea #23

Think of a number 1 through 8. Add 9 to the chosen number. Double the sum. Subtract 4. Divide by 2. Subtract the chosen number. What can you say about the answer using any number 1 through 8?

Think of a number 1 through 8. Multiply the number by 3. Add 1 to the product. Multiply the sum by 3. Add 8 to the product. What do you conclude?

Think of a number from 1 through 9. Add 1 and multiply by 3. Add 2 and multiply by 4. Add 1 and divide by 3. Add 1 and divide by 4. Subtract your original number. The answer is always the same. What is it?

Multiply the number 9 by any other number lower than 9. Subtract this product from 10 times your age. The first two digits plus the last digit gives you your age.

Idea #24

Make a four lane race track and divide it into sixteenths. Label 1/8, 1/4, 3/8, 1/2, 5/8, 3/4 and 7/8 for each inch. Make a spinner board with all fractions on it. Also make divisions on the spinner board entitled *Take An Extra Turn, Go Back Home* and *Lose One Turn.* Each child spins the spinner and moves as many spaces as indicated on the board. The first child to the end of the track is the winner.

Idea #25

Cut a piece of board two inches wide and seven inches long. Make nine holes equal distance apart. Place four white golf tees on one side and four red golf tees on the other side. The object of the game is to interchange the white tees and the red tees. The following rules apply: (1) The white tees must all move one way and the red ones the other. (2) You can move only one tee at a time. (3) You can move to an adjacent hole. (4) You can jump, but only one tee of the opposite color. If the children are having trouble with this game, use fewer tees.

Idea #26

Cut a piece of board two inches wide and six inches long. Place three pegs on the board equal distance apart. Place five metal washers on the middle peg, each slightly smaller than the next. Transfer the washers from the center peg to either of the other pegs, ending with the washers arranged in the same order as at the start. You may move only one washer at a time and a larger washer may never be placed on top of a smaller one.

Effective Use of the Tape Recorder

Few mechanical devices in the school will be of more use to the auxiliary than the tape recorder. Below are several creative ways the tape recorder can be used with children:

A. Tape the children's voices at intervals. This will make them aware that speaking skill is vital to later success.

B. Have the children take turns in reading a story into the tape recorder.

C. Use the tape recorder to tape things you want to share with parents.

D. Children are motivated to write original stories, poems, and songs when they can record them on tape. After the writing period, let them go back to the recorder one by one and record their writing. Playback will be fun.

E. Exercises where the child selects the correct form of the verb should be heard rather than read if real speech improvement is to take place. Have the children listen and indicate by a plus or minus whether or not the word was used correctly. Enunciation, verb tense, correct selection of words, proper word order, agreement of subject and predicate, proper use of adverbs and adjectives can all be tested.

F. Record sounds on tape. Use them for creative writing or creative dramatics.

G. Sometimes children get very excited when using a particular kind of equipment or engaging in a particularly exciting activity. Periodically tape some of these interesting happenings. It will make for some added excitement in the classroom and possibly give you material for creative writing.

H. Record puppet skits on your recorder. This gives you more time to manipulate the puppets.

I. Use the tape recorder to make dramatic presentations like phoning the fire department, police department, or witnessing something like a flying saucer. Evaluate the discussion later.

J. Prepare a radio broadcast on tape.

K. Use the tape recorder to evaluate things like class discussion, the teacher's presentation, and the behavior of the class. Evaluate when the session is over.

L. Record all sorts of interesting things around your community, like the demolition of an old building, the blastoff to the moon, sounds people make in department stores, etc. They can be used for creative writing or background for drama.

M. Tape resource people who come to class.

N. Interview unusual people like authors, window washers, old people, etc.

O. Have a tape exchange with another child in the school. Extend to the community, other communities, states, or other countries.

P. Tape bird calls. See if you can recognize the birds from the sounds they make.

Q. Record great speeches on television or radio. If the speech is a campaign speech, save it and compare it with what the candidate is saying a few months later.

S. Tape mathematical problems. Give the child ample time to solve the problem before going to the next.

T. Interview students who have just returned from a field trip.

A Word about Winning

You have probably noticed that most of the above games and activities can decide winners and losers. This may appear inconsistent with the rest of the book in that the emphasis has been upon a cooperative, helping relationship between members of the team and the interaction of the team with the child.

It should be made perfectly clear that although these activities can decide winners and losers, they need not. And if they do, it is assumed that it will be done in as humane a way as possible.

Bibliography of Effective Activities for Auxiliaries

Creative ideas are not in short supply. There is a constant stream of books and pamphlets that are helping auxiliary personnel unlock the creative potential of children. Below is a list of several good sources for creative ideas that cover the entire spectrum of the school curriculum.

Abbott, Jerry, *IDEAS: Newspaper in the Classroom* (Grand Forks, N.D., Grand Forks Herald, 1970)

Applegate, Mauree, *Easy in English* (Evanston, Ill., Harper and Row Publishers, Inc., 1960)

Applegate, Mauree, *Freeing Children to Write* (Evanston, Ill., Harper and Row Publishers, Inc., 1963)

Carlson, Ruth, *Writing Aides Through the Grades* (New York, N.Y., Teacher's College Press, Columbia University, 1970)

Ciotti, Rita and Ida Kravitz, *Independent Reading Activities* (Philadelphia, Pa., Great Cities Improvement Program, Philadelphia Board of Education)

Darrow, Helen and Virgil Howes, *Approaches to Individualized Reading* (New York, N.Y., Appleton Century Crofts, 1960)

Darrow, Helen and Roach Van Allen, *Independent Activities for Creative Learning,* New York, N.Y., Bureau of Publications, Teachers College, Columbia University, 1961)

Eckgren, Betty Lois, and Vivian Fishel, *500 Ideas for the Grade Teacher* (New York, N.Y., Harper and Row Publishers, Inc., 1952)

Educational Service Inc., *Spice* (Language Arts), *Probe* (Science), *Plus* (Mathematics), *Spark* (Social Studies), *Create* (Art), *Action* (Physical Education), *Stage* (Dramatics), *Rescue* (Remedial Reading), *Anchor* (Vocabulary Discovery), *Pride* (Black Studies), *Launch* (Early Learning), Stevensville, Michigan.

Gray, William, Monroe and Others, *Such Interesting Things to Do* (Chicago, Ill, Scott Foresman, Inc., 1963)

Herr, Selma, *Learning Activities for Reading* (Dubuque, Iowa, William C. Brown, Inc., 1961)

Herrick, Virgil and Marcella Nerbovig, *Using Experience Charts with Children* (Columbus, Ohio, Charles F. Merrill Publishing Co., 1964)

Hosier, Max and Mildred Blackman, *Listening Games: Building Skills with Instructional Games* (Darien, Conn., Grade Teacher Publication, Teachers Publishing Co., 1962)

Hurwitz, Abraham and Arthur Goddard, *Games to Improve Your Child's English* (New York, N.Y., Simon and Schuster, Inc., 1969)

Jackson, Doris and Dorothy Saunders, *They All Want to Write* (New York, N.Y., Holt, Rinehart and Winston, Inc., 1964)

Jensen, Amy Elizabeth, "Attracting Children to Books" (*Elementary English,* Vol. 33, pp. 332-39, 1956)

New York City Board of Education, *A Practical Guide to Individualized Reading* (New York, N.Y., Bureau of Educational Research, 1960)

Russell, David, *Let's Play a Game* (Chicago, Ill., Ginn and Company)

Russell, David and Elizabeth Russell, *Listening Aides Through the Grades* (New York, N.Y., Teacher College Press, Teacher's College, Columbia University, 1959)

Russell, David and Etta Karp, *Reading Aides Through the Grades* (New York, N.Y., Bureau of Publications, Teacher's College, Columbia University, 1961)

San Diego County Department of Education, *Self Selection Reading* (San Diego, Calif., 1966)

Sawicki, Florence, Janis Blakey, Eleanor Barnette and Geraldine Elliott, Key Words to Reading: *The Language Experience Approach Begins* (Tempe, Arizona, Arizona State University, 1969)

Smith, James, *Creative Teaching in the Elementary School Series: Language Arts, Reading and Literature, Creative Arts, Social Studies, Mathematics, Science, and Setting Conditions for Creative Teaching* (Boston, Mass., Allyn and Bacon, Inc., 1967)

Van Allen, Roach and Claryce Van Allen, *Language Experiences in Reading, Levels I, II, and III* (Chicago, Ill., Encyclopedia Britannica Press, 1969)

Van Allen, Roach, and Doris Lee, *Learning to Read Through Experience* (New York, N.Y., Educational Division, Meredith Corporation, Appleton Century Crofts, 1963)

Veatch, Jeanette, *Reading in the Elementary School* (New York, N.Y., Ronald Press, 1966)

Wagner, Guy, Edna Christophel and Laura Gilloley, *Social Studies Games and Activities* (Darien, Conn., Teacher College Corporation, 1968)

Wagner, Guy and Max Hosier, *Reading Games: Strengthening Reading Skills with Instructional Games* (Darien, Conn., Grade Teacher Publications, 1960)

Willcox, Isabel, *Language Arts Activities for the Independent Work Period* (Englewood Cliffs, N.J., Teacher's College Practical Press, Inc., (Prentice-Hall) Educational Series, 1963)

Willcox, Isabel, *120 Activities for the Independent Work Period* (Englewood Cliffs, N.J., Prentice-Hall, Inc., 1963)

Learning is so much fun
when you make a game of it.

Figure 7-1

When things get tough we call in the teacher.

Summary

So often you hear teachers criticize the use of games and creative activities on the ground they are paid to *teach* and not entertain. "Why can't we present the material as we used to? The children seemed to learn pretty well under that system."

What some of them have forgotten is that the societal values are changing so rapidly it is hardly within our comprehension. Phenomenal changes are taking place in our culture that absolutely demand that educational techniques be different.

Increased leisure time, television, technology, transcience, the explosion of knowledge, and world travel are examples of why it is now justifiable to seek more effective ways in the classroom.

The activities in this chapter are presented with the intent they will be a springboard to even better, more creative ways to excite children about learning.

Chapter 8

The Principal and
the Teacher's Team

"I would like to do it, but the principal won't allow it." How many times have you heard that?

When analyzing that statement, a couple of thoughts come to mind. First, many teachers are using that as a convenient barricade against change. Second, there are supervisors, and their numbers are large enough to be embarrassing to the profession, that desire the status quo, and have great fears about venturing into the unknown.

Studies continually report that the quality of the school is directly related to the quality of the leader.

Witness:

> A recent study by the Center for the Advanced Study of Educational Administration at the University of Oregon found the problems facing elementary principals are leading to a leadership crisis that is seriously endangering the future of elementary education in this country. Their conclusion was that large allocations of time, money, and the best educational resources must be pumped into the problems of the principalship if quality programs are to be implemented. An interview of 300

principals disclosed that they want to become leaders, but lack the skills to know what to do. The study notes that most of the problems identified by principals involve their difficulty in establishing and maintaining successful human relationships and lack of knowledge of the strategies to employ in effecting educational change.[1]

Witness:

A recent study of the New York City schools by an independent non-school agency tried to determine priorities for the spending of school monies. In a sample of fourteen Black/Puerto Rican schools, they interviewed the principals to see if there was any correlation between administrative role and the teaching of reading. A School Quality Index was derived and seems to explain the percentage of variation in reading score improvement in the sample.

This is what they found. Significant improvements in reading skills were associated with a principal's belief that he had a competent professional staff in the fourth and fifth grades, respected his teachers' aides working in the classroom and used them extensively, had meaningful parent and community involvement in the school, and practiced or supported innovative administration or teaching techniques. Relative backsliding in achievement was associated with opposite attitudes.

Even if the high coefficient of correlation is discounted somewhat because of the subjectivity necessarily involved in translating attitudes (qualitative) into a numerical index (quantitative), the resulting numbers appear to be, at the least, provocative.

Two elements appear to be at work in those schools that yielded the high correlations. First of all, a school which manages to involve the total environment of the child into the educational process has more resources, both tangible and intangible, available for education than a school that does not. Second, for a combination of these factors to be operating, the staff, the community, and the children must have respect for themselves and the other participants in the school.[2]

---

[1] *Elementary Principals and Their Schools* (Eugene, Ore.: Center for the Advanced Study of Educational Administration, 1972), pp. 8-9.

[2] Donald Mitchell and Anne Hawley, *Leadership in Public Education: A Look at the Overlooked* (Washington, D.C.: Academy for Educational Development, Inc., 1972), p. 13.

The Call to Lead

The problem is pretty well defined, and the answer seems clear—either principals diligently learn new skills or practices in schools will remain the same.

The principalship is very demanding. To be accountable to children, their parents, teachers, other principals, the central office, the school board, and the public at large is no easy task. It requires a person of great energy, vision and temperament.

The acronym ACTION has already been used as a way to identify these many dimensions. To change a school without first changing the role of the teacher is to violate the rule which says that good schools have high morale and good human relations (Auxiliary Program). If one believes that good schools have good leaders, every school will have a well planned program of supervision that places group decision making and self-assessment at its heart (Cooperative Supervision). When all facets of the school program are working in harmony, one with the other, individualized instruction for each pupil becomes a reality (Teaching and Learning). To strike out into areas unknown to parents is to make the job twice as difficult as when you have the support and help of parents (Involvement of the Community). Good schools of today are very concerned about how children are organized for instruction. A visionary leader and his staff, concerned about making school more like the real world and more success oriented, will seek organizational patterns away from those of the past which have little relevance to the real world(Organization of the School). All forward looking leaders understand that any innovative endeavor always brings people into closer human relationships with each other, and thus the need for programs that help all school personnel find the entwining relationship (Nurturing Humaneness).

How the Principal Relates to the Teacher's Team

The key to the implementation of the Teacher's Team is the building principal, for it is he who will either blunt innovation or cause it to flourish.

The Auxiliary Program

The evidence pours in; teachers are spending about one-half of their time doing things that could better be performed by someone with far less training and experience. Only when administrators begin to internalize this will the teachers begin to devote more of their time to the individualizing of instruction.

Sit down with your staff and ask them for feedback about how they are perceiving their role. You will probably be shocked when you discover how much you ask of them is peripheral to the main task of individualizing instruction for each child. Set a goal that no teacher will be allowed to do any clerical work and then proceed as if that goal can be accomplished. You will be surprised how rapidly the idea will be picked up by the staff and how quickly an auxiliary program will develop. The staff will love you for it and people who never had time to think about innovative practices will suddenly appear in your office and want some ideas about changing the environment of the room, individualizing instruction, or beginning a program of community involvement.

Tutors

You simply cannot help but be impressed by the research on tutors. All over this country innovative teachers and their principals are experimenting with the use of youth tutoring youth, and in nearly every case they report fantastic attitudinal and academic increases.

Lowering the pupil-teacher ratio is a well-known method of producing positive effects, but there are other dynamics surrounding tutors that are producing some very significant changes in schools. The caring, sharing relationship, a relationship that seems increasingly difficult to maintain in our culture, is profoundly evident when children tutor other children. And the hierarchy, a part of our culture that continually gets in our way, also seems to break down. Equality seems to permeate the school. The teachers are just teachers. The intermediate teacher is no longer respected only because she teaches older children, and the kindergarten teacher the one you listen to only if you are a kindergarten child. And children seem to have a new respect for each other, a relationship very difficult' to maintain in the traditional school setting where different age children rarely mix.

You might begin by reading some ERIC abstracts on the subject of tutoring. You will be amazed how positive the research is on this subject. Then visit with teachers and administrators who have had some success with tutors. Ask them for some help in establishing guidelines for your program. Then just dive into the program and see how rapidly you meet success.

Community Involvement

Increasingly, community involvement is becoming a larger part of the responsibility of the school principal. It is now more time consuming because community involvement, or the direct involvement of parents in the school program, has replaced public relations, a term far more general and often implied to mean keeping the public informed.

If you deemphasize this part of the school program children will suffer, because their parents represent a tremendous talent bank. As important, especially if you value your mental health, to embark upon the path of innovation without involving parents is tantamount to burrs under the saddle of a bucking horse.

The principal cannot carry the program of community involvement. It takes committed staff members who understand the dynamics of change. Together with the staff, try to draw up a position statement on what could constitute a good program of community involvement. Guidelines and ideas are included in this book in abundance. Basically, the responsibility of the school administrator is to:

A. Cooperatively draw up guidelines;
B. Implement the program;
C. Support staff efforts with a constant input of ideas;
D. Summarize those techniques and share them with staff;
E. Give the program an on-going impetus.

Try some of the many ideas found in this book. As you begin to involve parents in the education of their children, both staff and parents will find a relationship with each other that heretofore did not exist.

Accountability is on the lips of every teacher and administrator in America. And there aren't many faces smiling as they say that word. In fact, it is a word that is causing considerable distress.

Maybe part of the answer to accountability lies in the program of community involvement; a situation in which school people feel so good about themselves they are not afraid to encourage parents to participate in the education of their children. Which method of accountability do you prefer?

Reporting Pupil Progress

How do you report pupil progress to parents? This is a very vital question because your success in involving parents in the education of their children is directly related to your success in reporting pupil progress in a meaningful way.

Do you think parents will feel good enough about themselves and their children to work in the school if their children are continually judged? Absolutely not, for when you judge the child you also judge his parents. So when your reporting is negative in nature, that is, you call or write when there is trouble, only one thing can result—a situation where parents shudder each time they receive a report from the child's teacher.

This book has tried to establish the fact that there is no longer any utility in failing children. Considering the danger in that statement, without qualifying it, please refer to the chapter on reporting to parents. Build success into your school program and report that success to your parents. Then and only then will they accept your invitation to be an integral part of the school.

Ideas for Effective Teaching

A section on effective ideas has been included because of the necessity of providing success experiences for auxiliaries. To ask them to teach out of the same, oftentimes dull, basals that we use is to discourage them and decrease their chances of success.

It is the responsibility of the principal to keep a steady flow of ideas pumped into his teaching staff. They are available in huge numbers and all that is needed is one who is excited about the possibilities of teaching children in this new exciting way.

And if this applies to children, it also applies to teachers. Are you still calling busy teachers together in large groups and lecturing to them about the latest educational innovations? If you are, you may soon have no audience.

Teachers, contrary to popular opinion, do not mind participating in in-service activities. What they do mind is to participate in one meeting after another that has no relevance to their day-to-day activities.

The next time you think about an in-service meeting, try the games approach. Make up a booklet of twenty or so of the ideas for games found in this book. Bring some examples of each. Talk for five minutes and let them go to work. You can just see the attitudinal change as they begin to realize that for the first time they have had something to take back to their classroom that will help them excite children about learning. Now that these techniques work so well with the staff, use them more often with the children and see if they don't get turned on about learning in a way in which they never did before.

The Principal's Team

One of the greatest problems facing principals today is the warring camps that have surfaced as a result of educational innovation. Twenty years ago this was not a problem because schools were much alike. All of the schools of a given system used the same curriculum guides, taught in the same way, followed the same organizational patterns, and were administered according to the same procedures.

Presently, there is rapid movement away from these practices. A new breed of teachers and administrators, cultural changes, and parents demanding educational alternatives for their children have no doubt been the contributing factors.

This has been very positive from the standpoint of innovation, but very destructive of human relations. Administrators in the same system are now competing with each other in a way that is sometimes good, but many times bad. Instead of cooperation and sharing we have competition and hoarding. Something needs to be done or another leadership crisis, yet unstudied, will lift its ugly head.

Most often principals are assigned to one building, or if the school district is looking for ways to cut administrative costs they will be assigned to two buildings. There are also times when the school unit is so small that it cannot economically be justified to have a full time principal in the building. Whatever the case, it is now time to look at other ways of assigning principals to make the maximum use of their creative energy.

Principal Intern Programs

One way to make the most of a system's talent bank is to implement an intern program. In this type of arrangement one principal is responsible for two or more buildings and at the same time he is supervising the staff, he is training principal interns who do much of the administrative work. The advantage of this type of arrangement is that administrative competencies can be spread over a greater number of children and teachers, the system now has an opportunity to train its own administrators, and a think tank possibility emerges as a result of several people attacking problems collectively.

For two years I was project director of a principal intern program called Principal-In-Training. I was the principal of two schools the first year and four the next. Three principal interns were assigned to me. Presently two of these interns are principals. I continue to be impressed by the relationship that was established between us as a result of this experience. Even though we are no longer involved in the program, we still plan together and share in a way unique to the principalship.

As I view this relationship, and the one that is fostered in the one principal in one building arrangement, I cannot help but conclude that under the traditional arrangement I could have a twin brother administering a school across the street, our families could be the best of friends, and at the end of forty years we would still know little about each other's operation.

Will that break the warring camps? Maybe not. Maybe nothing will. At least it will begin to develop a sharing relationship that cannot help but be worthwhile for children.

Ad Hoc Administration

Alvin Toffler, in his book *Future Shock,* describes the coming ad-hocracy in which the typical hierarchial methods of decision making are no longer working. The acceleration of change due to a highly transient and technological society is now calling for new approaches to decision making. With respect to the present methods, Toffler says, traditional functional organization structures, created to meet predictable, non-novel conditions, prove incapable of responding effectively to radical changes in the environment.[3]

So the ladder type of decision making is now being replaced by a more functional system. Leaders of the future will be grouped around tasks, and only for as long as the need exists. It may be a few months, a few weeks, or even a few days. When the problem has been solved, the group will disband and form again around another task or set of problems.

Industry has already shifted to this type of process because they found themselves using a structure designed to solve problems that no longer existed.[4] In a recent three year period, sixty-six of the nation's one hundred largest industries reported major organizational shake-ups.[5]

In comparing the decision making process of both the bureaucracy and the adhocracy, Toffler makes this interesting comparison:

Organization Man of the Bureaucracy	*Associative Man of the Ad-hocracy*
1. Subservient to the organization	1. Nonchalant about the organization
2. Great concern for economic security	2. Takes economic security for granted
3. Fears risk	3. Welcomes risk
4. Hierarchy conscious, seeks status inside the organization	4. Little concern for the hierarchy, seeks status outside the organization
5. Fills a predetermined slot in the organization	5. Moves from slot to slot in the organization
6. Solution of problems according to a well-defined set of rules	6. Novel problems encourage innovation
7. Subordinates his own individuality to play ball on the team	7. Recognizes the transience of the team and will not subordinate his individuality for any length of time[6]

Figure 8-1

---

[3]Alvin Toffler, *Future Shock* (New York, N.Y.: Random House, Inc., 1970), p. 135.

[4]Toffler, *Future Shock*, p. 131.

[5]Toffler, *Future Shock*, p. 129.

[6]Toffler, *Future Shock*, pp. 149-150.

When you look at the way schools are organized for decision making you cannot help but be impressed by the fact that we, too, are the victims of a highly transient world. In the not too distant future, administrators may not be assigned to buildings on a permanent basis. Rather, they will be part of a task force whose job it is to identify problems and form highly flexible, fluid groups in order to solve those problems.

The coming ad-hocracy will call for people to be more adaptable than ever before. The rapid turnover of people, places and things will create problems that haven't even been thought of yet. But the price all of us will pay for becoming the Associative Man will be small compared to what it will be like trying to administer a structure designed to solve problems that no longer exist.

The Principal and School-Wide Decision Making

Maximum effectiveness of the Teacher's Team will become reality only if the school principal allows his staff and his community the power of shared decision making. This concept, although quite new in education, is gathering momentum in industry.

In the July 17, 1972 issue of *U.S. News and World Report,* in an article entitled, "The Drive to Make Dull Jobs Interesting," it was reported that industry is now injecting interest and incentives into daily chores by allowing workers to make many of the decisions that affect them. Among the innovations are:

> An auto-parts plant in Holland, Michigan let workers decide how fast to run the production line, and when to shut it down for a rest period. Employees also determine their own pay increases.
>
> Textile-machine operators in a Pensacola, Florida mill can move from one job to another from day to day.
>
> Each worker at an instrument plant in Medfield, Massachusetts used to install a separate part in products on the assembly line. Now, to make jobs more challenging, the individual worker assembles complete instruments.
>
> Employees in a huge new appliance factory near Columbia, Maryland participate in give-and-take sessions with management on job-related questions and problems.
>
> At a food processing plant in Topeka, Kansas workers on production, office and shipping teams shift jobs on a rotating

schedule, a system that has boosted output and cut production costs sharply.[7]

The main idea behind such a change in procedures is that of trying to move authority and responsibility downward to a level of the hierarchy that is most capable of making decisions.

Industry has taken a bold new step in giving the workers something to say about decisions that affect them. It has resulted in increased production and high morale among the employees.

It is now time that educators follow industry by allowing both parents and their children some input into the decision making process. Too many decisions are being made by people who oftentimes have little knowledge upon which to base that decision.

The wise principal will consider moving the decision making process down to the level of the hierarchy most capable of making that decision. At times he will make the decision himself with little or no input from the staff. At other times he will consult staff members, parents and their children.

It is recommended that team leaders become part of an internal committee for decision making if the school happens to be organized around team teaching. If the school is self-contained, as most are, some other method will be needed to select members for this committee. Whatever the case, the important thing is that each school form a committee for decision making, being careful not to exclude parents and children, in such a way as to allow all concerned some power of determining the direction of the school.

What kind of problems would this committee attack? If you really believe that decisions should be moved to that level of the hierarchy most capable of making them, you would consider the following kinds of problems for this committee:

1. School-wide curriculum improvement;
2. School-wide goals;
3. School-wide problems of administration that affect all staff and students;
4. Guidelines for the use of time, space, equipment and personnel;
5. School-wide evaluation;
6. Priorities for the expenditure of monies.

---

[7]"The Drive to Make Dull Jobs Interesting," *U.S. News and World Report*, Vol. LXXIII, No. 3, July 17, 1972, p. 50.

Summary

There is a current trend among some educational writers to hang the label of gatekeeper upon all administrators. They see the school principal as one who frustrates innovation. Herbert Kohl, author of *The Open Classroom,* recommended that teachers keep two sets of lesson plans, one for the supervisor that follows the curriculum and another for oneself that deals with the reality of one's classroom.[8] Will instructional improvement ever take place under those conditions? I think not.

The time is now right for all school staff, the students, and the community to team and share decision making in such a way as to enlarge all concerned. Then and only then will we realize that elusive goal of individualized instruction for all children and a full measure of humaneness for every human being.

---

[8]Herbert Kohl, *The Open Classroom* (New York, N.Y.: Random House, Inc., 1969), p. 91.

A Final Word

Where does the answer to instructional improvement lie? I think it lies in *The Auxiliary Teacher Program.* Only when the professional staff begins to realize the great potential now untapped, and begins to use them in a meaningful way, will we have significant improvement in schools.

Not long ago I visited a very innovative elementary school. This school was not a new school, nor was it equipped with all of the latest technology. On the contrary, it was a very old school and the technology was the creative energy of the teachers and children.

This school had atmosphere such as you will never see anywhere. Why? Because the children and teachers had such a relevant program and the children had so much pride in the school they just couldn't help but share that pride with visitors.

Almost everywhere I looked I saw a creative use of resources, both human and nonhuman. The nonhuman aspect of the program was a huge mass of learning games, most of which had been made by children and teachers.

But what is a teacher? In that school it was the professionals and their supportive staff. Everywhere you looked you could see a *teacher* with a small group of three or four children.

And the visitors begin to whisper. "We could do this too if we had all this staff . . . look at all the staff they have!" So they ask the principal where he got all of his staff.

As he begins to tell his story you know that he understands *The Auxiliary Teacher Program.* He talks of the regular professional staff. They are organized into teams with a leader. And he talks of the creative use of Title I personnel; how he is using the vast amount of personnel available from the university; how children are teaching other children; how parents are being used in the classroom, and how businessmen have cooperated in a Career Awareness Program that takes children to their places of business and brings the businessmen into the school.

Are you waiting for the central office to staff your school? If you are, you will probably wait a long time. They can only do so much; the rest is up to you.

Bibliography

Abbott, Jerry L. *Meet the Auxiliary Personnel at J. Nelson Kelly Elementary School,* Grand Forks, North Dakota, 1967.

Abbott, Jerry L. "Improving Instruction With Teacher Aides" *North Dakota Journal of Education,* Vol. XLIX, May, 1970, pp. 10-12.

Gallup, George. "Third Annual Survey of Parent Attitudes About the Public Schools" *Phi Delta Kappan,* September, 1971, pp. 33-48.

Harris, Thomas. *I'm OK You're OK,* New York, N.Y.: Harper and Row Publishers, Inc., 1967.

Laurie, Ellen. *How to Change the Schools: A Parent's Handbook on How to Fight the System,* New York, N.Y.: Random House, Inc., 1970.

National Commission on Resources for Youth, Inc. *Supervisors Manual: Youth Tutoring Youth,* New York, N.Y., 1968.

Palmer, Richard. "Teacher Aides Under Glass" *North Dakota Journal of Education,* March, 1968, pp. 19-21.

Warner, Sylvia-Ashton. *Teacher,* New York, N.Y.: Simon & Schuster, Inc., 1963.

Wartenberg, Milton. *Auxiliary Personnel in Education Series,* Units One Through Eight. Chicago, Illinois: Science Research Associates, Inc., 1967.

Index